W9-BMO-122

Best of Ruby Quiz

Volume One

Best of Ruby Quiz
Volume One

James Edward Gray II

The Pragmatic Bookshelf
Raleigh, North Carolina   Dallas, Texas

Many of the designations used by manufacturers and sellers to distinguish their products are claimed as trademarks. Where those designations appear in this book, and The Pragmatic Programmers, LLC was aware of a trademark claim, the designations have been printed in initial capital letters or in all capitals. The Pragmatic Starter Kit, The Pragmatic Programmer, Pragmatic Programming, Pragmatic Bookshelf and the linking *g* device are trademarks of The Pragmatic Programmers, LLC.

Every precaution was taken in the preparation of this book. However, the publisher assumes no responsibility for errors or omissions, or for damages that may result from the use of information (including program listings) contained herein.

Our Pragmatic courses, workshops, and other products can help you and your team create better software and have more fun. For more information, as well as the latest Pragmatic titles, please visit us at

> http://www.pragmaticprogrammer.com

ISBN 0-9766940-7-7

Printed on acid-free paper with 85% recycled, 30% post-consumer content.

First printing, February 2006

Version: 2006-2-14

Contents

II Answers and Discussion 69

Chapter 1

Introduction

If you stop and think about it, programming knowledge is nearly useless by itself. What exactly are you going to create with all that expert programming skill, if it's all you have? The world needs only so many text editors.

What makes the craft interesting is how we apply it. Combine programming prowess with accounting practices or even just a need to reunite hurricane victims with their scattered family members, and you have the makings of a real, and potentially useful, application.

Practical programming experience can be surprisingly hard to come by. There are classes and books to give us theory and syntax. If you've been a programmer for any amount of time, you will have read plenty of those books. Then what? I think most of us inherently know that the next step is to write something, but many of us struggle to find a topic.

I love games. I'm always playing something, and struggling to put together a winning strategy never quite feels like work to me. I use that to make myself a better programmer. I play games with my code.

I assign myself a task I've never tried before, perhaps to get more familiar with an algorithm or a library. Or sometimes I'll give myself a completely routine task but add an unusual twist: implement this full-featured trivial program in one hour or less.

This is my form of practice for the big game. I find what works and even what doesn't.[1] I memorize idioms I like, just in case I run into a

---

[1] True story: I'm still struggling with one programming problem I've been playing with for about ten years now. I've never found a solution I like, though I know others have solved it. (I haven't peeked!) I also haven't made it a Ruby Quiz yet, because I'm not ready to be embarrassed. I'll get it eventually....

similar problem down the road. All the while, I'm getting more familiar with languages, libraries, and frameworks I may need to work with someday.

The set of weekly programming challenges for the Ruby programming language called Ruby Quiz[2] was born out of my desire to share this with the rest of the world. This book holds some highlights from the first year of its run.

What's Inside

In these pages, you will find a collection of problems contributed by myself and others to enhance your programming knowledge. The great thing about working with these problems is that they come with discussions on some of their interesting points and sample solutions from other programmers. You can solve the challenges and then compare and contrast your code with the solutions provided.

There is not yet a way to download all of these programming idioms directly into your brain. Let me forewarn you, solving these problems is work.[3] We try to have fun with the Ruby Quiz, but it doesn't come without the price of a little effort. The problems vary in difficulty, but I believe there's something to be learned from all of them.

How to Use This Book

This book isn't meant for passive readers! Get those brain cells moving. You will learn a lot more by giving a quiz your best shot, even if it doesn't blossom into a solution, and then reading the discussions. It's the context you gain from the attempt that allows you to internalize what you learn, and that's the whole point.

May this teach you half of what it has taught me.

Finding Your Way Around

The front of this book is a collection of twenty-five programming challenges. In the back of the book, you can find discussions and solutions

---

[2]http://rubyquiz.com
[3]Yes, I'm one of the guys who skips the "Additional Exercises" in almost all programming books. However, I must admit that I've learned the most when I actually did them.

for these problems. The separation is there to allow you to scan problems and find something you want to try without accidentally running into a spoiler. At the beginning of each quiz, you will find a pointer to the page the relevant discussion begins on.

Along the way you will find:

Live Code

Most of the code snippets shown within come from full-length, running examples, which you can download.[4] To help you find your way, if code can be found in the download, there'll be a marker line like the one that follows at the top of the listing in the book:

```
code/madlibs/parsed_madlib.rb
# Ordinary prose.
class String
  # Anything is acceptable.
  def self.parse?( token, replacements )
    new(token)
  end
end
```

If you're reading the PDF version of this book and if your PDF viewer supports hyperlinks, you can click the marker, and the code should appear in a browser window. Some browsers (such as Safari) might mistakenly try to interpret some of the code as HTML. If this happens, view the source of the page to see the real source code.

Joe Asks...

Joe, the mythical developer, sometimes pops up to ask questions about stuff we talk about in the text. We try to answer these as we go along.

Spring Cleaning

Solutions in this text are just as they were submitted originally, with the following exceptions:

- Tabs have been replaced with the Ruby standard practice of two spaces.

- Method and variable names were adjusted to Ruby's *snake_case* style convention.

---

[4]From http://pragmaticprogrammer.com/titles/fr_quiz/code.html

- Obvious minor bugs have been fixed.

- Some class definitions were split up into smaller pieces just to make them easier to present to the reader.

- The text has been edited for grammar and spelling.

Any other changes will be called out in the margin of the code listings as they occur.

Who Really Made All of This

So many people contributed to this book, I can hardly take credit for writing it. I will call out contributions of problems and code as they come up, but that's such a small part of the story. Ruby Quiz simply wouldn't exist if it wasn't for all the wonderful contributors who have shared problems, ideas, and discussions since I started the project. Together, they have created a sensational community resource while I mostly just watched it happen. I am eternally grateful to the entire Ruby Quiz community.

The second side of my support base is the most fantastic bunch of family and friends a guy could have. They truly make me believe I can do anything. Without them I would be merely mortal.

Finally, but most important, I must thank Dana, my true inspiration. You believed long before I did, and as always, you were right. Here is the proof.

Part I

The Quizzes

Mad Libs

This Ruby Quiz is to write a program that presents the user with that favorite childhood game, Mad Libs. Don't worry if you have never played; it's an easy game to learn. A Mad Libs is a story with several placeholders. For example:

```
I had a ((an adjective)) sandwich for lunch today.  It dripped all
over my ((a body part)) and ((a noun)).
```

The reader, the only person who sees the story, will ask another person for each placeholder in turn and record the answers. In this example, they would ask for an adjective, a body part, and a noun. The reader then reads the story, with the answers in place. It might come out something like this:

```
I had a smelly sandwich for lunch today.  It dripped all
over my big toe and bathtub.
```

Laughter ensues.

The script should play the role of reader, asking the user for a series of words, then replacing placeholders in the story with the user's answers.

We'll keep our story format very simple, using a ((...)) notation for place-holders. Here's an example:

```
Our favorite language is ((a gemstone)).
```

If your program is fed that template, it should ask you to enter "a gemstone" and then display your version of the story:

```
Our favorite language is Ruby.
```

That covers the simple cases, but in some instances we may want to reuse an answer. For that, we'll introduce a way to name them:

```
Our favorite language is ((gem:a gemstone)).  We think ((gem)) is
better than ((a gemstone)).
```

With the previous story, your program should ask for two gemstones, then substitute the one designated by ((gem:...)) at ((gem)). When there is a colon in the ((...)), the part before the colon becomes the pointer to the reusable value, and the part after the colon is the prompt for the value. That would give results like this:

```
Our favorite language is Ruby.  We think Ruby is better than
Emerald.
```

You can choose any interface you like, as long as a user can interact with the end result. You can play around with a CGI-based solution at the Ruby Quiz site.[5] You can find the two Mad Libs files I'm using on the Ruby Quiz site as well.[6]

---

[5]http://rubyquiz.com/cgi-bin/madlib.cgi

[6]http://rubyquiz.com/madlibs/Lunch_Hungers.madlib and
http://rubyquiz.com/madlibs/Gift_Giving.madlib

LCD Numbers

This quiz is to write a program that displays LCD-style numbers at adjustable sizes.

The digits to be displayed will be passed as an argument to the program. Size should be controlled with the command-line option -s followed by a positive integer. The default value for -s is 2.

For example, if your program is called with this:

```
$ lcd.rb 012345
```

the correct display is this:

```
 --        --   --        --
|  |    |    |    | |  | |
|  |    |  --| __| |__| |__
|  |    | |    |    |    |
|__|    | |__  __|    |  __|
```

And for this:

```
> lcd.rb -s 1 6789
```

your program should print this:

Note the single column of space between digits in both examples. For other values of -s, simply lengthen the - and | bars.

Quiz **3**
Answer on page 87

GEDCOM Parser

Posed by Jamis Buck

GEDCOM is the "GEnealogical Data COMmunication" file format. It is a plain-text electronic format used to transfer genealogical data.[7] The purpose of this quiz is to develop a simple parser that can convert a GEDCOM file to XML.

GEDCOM Format

The GEDCOM file format is very straightforward.Each line represents a node in a tree. It looks something like this:

```
0 @I1@ INDI
1 NAME Jamis Gordon /Buck/
2 SURN Buck
2 GIVN Jamis Gordon
1 SEX M
...
```

In general, each line is formatted like this:

```
LEVEL TAG-OR-ID [DATA]
```

The LEVEL is an integer, representing the current depth in the tree. If subsequent lines have greater levels than the current node, they are children of the current node.

TAG-OR-ID is a tag that identifies the type of data in that node, or it is a unique identifier. Tags are three- or four-letter words in uppercase. The unique identifiers are always text surrounded by @ characters (such as @I54@). If an ID is given, the DATA is the type of the subtree that is identified.

---

[7]We're not concerned here with whether it is a particularly *good* file format. It is certainly more compact than the corresponding XML would be, and bandwidth was particularly important back when the standard was developed.

So, to take apart the example given previously, you have this:

- 0 @I1@ INDI. This starts a new subtree of type INDI ("individual"). The ID for this individual is *@I1@*.

- 1 NAME Jamis Gordon /Buck/. This starts a NAME subtree with a value of Jamis Gordon /Buck/.

- 2 SURN Buck. This is a subelement of the NAME subtree, of type SURN ("surname").

- 2 GIVN Jamis Gordon. Same as SURN but specifies the given name of the individual.

- 1 SEX M. Creates a new sub-element of the INDI element, of type SEX (i.e., "gender").

And so forth.

Variable whitespace is allowed between the level and the tag. Blank lines are ignored.

The Challenge

The challenge is to create a parser that takes a GEDCOM file as input and converts it to XML. The snippet of GEDCOM given previously would become the following:

```
<gedcom>
  <indi id="@I1@">
    <name>
      Jamis Gordon /Buck/
      <surn>Buck</surn>
      <givn>Jamis Gordon</givn>
    </name>
    <sex>M</sex>
    . . .
  </indi>
  . . .
</gedcom>
```

Sample Input

There is a large GEDCOM file online[8] containing the lineage of various European royalty. This particular file makes generous use of white-space to increase readability.

---

[8]http://www.rubyquiz.com/royal.ged

Quiz **4**
Answer on page 93

Animal Quiz

Posed by Jim Weirich

Here's an animal quiz program to try as a Ruby Quiz.

It works like this: The program starts by telling the user to think of an animal. It then begins asking a series of yes/no questions about that animal: Does it swim? Does it have hair? And so on.... Eventually, it will narrow down the possibilities to a single animal and guess: is it a mouse?

If the program has guessed correctly, the game is over and may be restarted with a new animal. If the program has guessed incorrectly, it asks the user for the kind of animal they were thinking of and then asks for the user to provide a question that can distinguish between its incorrect guess and the correct answer. It then adds the new question and animal to its "database" and will guess that animal in the future (if appropriate). Your program should remember what it has learned between runs.

Here's a sample run:

```
⇒    Think of an animal...
     Is it an elephant?  (y or n)
⇐    n
⇒    You win.  Help me learn from my mistake before you go...
     What animal were you thinking of?
⇐    a rabbit
⇒    Give me a question to distinguish a rabbit from an elephant.
⇐    Is it a small animal?
⇒    For a rabbit, what is the answer to your question?  (y or n)
⇐    y
⇒    Thanks.
     Play again?  (y or n)
⇐    y
⇒    Think of an animal...
```

```
        Is it a small animal?  (y or n)
 ⇐      y
 ⇒      Is it a rabbit?  (y or n)
 ⇐      n
 ⇒      You win.  Help me learn from my mistake before you go...
        What animal were you thinking of?
 ⇐      a Shih Tzu
 ⇒      Give me a question to distinguish a Shih Tzu from a rabbit.
 ⇐      Is it a kind of dog?
 ⇒      For a Shih Tzu, what is the answer to your question?  (y or n)
 ⇐      y
 ⇒      Thanks.
        Play again?  (y or n)
 ⇐      y
 ⇒      Think of an animal...
        Is it a small animal?  (y or n)
 ⇐      y
 ⇒      Is it a kind of dog?  (y or n)
 ⇐      y
 ⇒      Is it a Shih Tzu?  (y or n)
 ⇐      y
 ⇒      I win.  Pretty smart, aren't I?
        Play again?  (y or n)
 ⇐      n
```

Quiz **5**
Answer on page 101

Scrabble Stems

Posed by Martin DeMello

In Scrabble[9] parlance, a *bingo* is a play where one gets rid of all seven letters. A *bingo stem* is a set of six letters that combine with another letter of the alphabet to make a seven-letter word. Some six-letter stems have more possible combinations than others. For instance, one of the more prolific stems, *SATIRE*, combines with twenty letters: *A*, *B*, *C*, *D*, *E*, *F*, *G*, *H*, *I*, *K*, *L*, *M*, *N*, *O*, *P*, *R*, *S*, *T*, *V*, and *W* to form words such as *ASTERIA*, *BAITERS*, *RACIEST*, and so on.

Write a program that, given a word list and a cutoff n, finds all six-letter stems that combine with n or more distinct letters, sorted by greatest number of combinations to least.

If you need a word list to help in developing a solution, you can find Spell Checking Oriented Word Lists (SCOWL) online.[10]

---

[9]A popular word game by Hasbro
[10]http://wordlist.sourceforge.net/

Regexp.build()

This quiz is to build a library that adds a class method called build() to Regexp and that should accept a variable number of arguments, which can include Integers and Ranges of Integers. Have build() return a Regexp object that will match only Integers in the set of passed arguments.

Here are some examples of possible usage:

```
lucky = Regexp.build(3, 7)
"7"    =~ lucky    # => true
"13"   =~ lucky    # => false
"3"    =~ lucky    # => true

month = Regexp.build(1..12)
"0"    =~ month    # => false
"1"    =~ month    # => true
"12"   =~ month    # => true

day = Regexp.build(1..31)
"6"    =~ day      # => true
"16"   =~ day      # => true
"Tues" =~ day      # => false

year = Regexp.build(98, 99, 2000..2005)
"04"   =~ year     # => false
"2004" =~ year     # => true
"99"   =~ year     # => true

num = Regexp.build(0..1_000_000)
"-1"   =~ num      # => false
```

You can determine the specifics of the expressions produced by your library. Here are issues you may want to consider:

• How should leading zeros be handled? For example, how would you handle matching the hour from a clock formatted in military time[11] (0 to 23), if hours 0 through 9 may or may not have a single leading zero?

- Should anything be captured by the returned Regexp?

- How should anchoring work?

```
"2004" =~ Regexp.build(4)    # => ???
```

---

[11]Also known as *24-hour time*

Quiz 7
Answer on page 113

HighLine

When you stop to think about it, methods such as gets(), while handy, are still pretty low level. In running Ruby Quiz I'm always seeing solutions with helper methods similar to this one from Markus König:

```ruby
code/highline/example.rb
def ask(prompt)
  loop do
    print prompt, ' '
    $stdout.flush
    s = gets
    exit if s == nil
    s.chomp!
    if s == 'y' or s == 'yes'
      return true
    elsif s == 'n' or s == 'no'
      return false
    else
      $stderr.puts "Please answer yes or no."
    end
  end
end
```

Surely we can make something like that better! We don't always need a web or GUI framework, and there's no reason writing a command-line application can't be equally smooth.

This Ruby Quiz is to start a module called HighLine (for *high*-level, *line*-oriented interface). Ideally this module would eventually cover many aspects of terminal interaction, but for this quiz we'll focus just on getting input.

What I really think we need here is to take a page out of the OptionParser book.[12] Here are some general ideas:

---

[12] At http://www.ruby-doc.org/stdlib/libdoc/optparse/rdoc/index.html

```
age = ask("What is your age?", Integer, :within => 0..105)
num = eval "0b#{ ask('Enter a binary number.',
                     String, :validate => /^[01_]+$/ ) }"

if ask_if("Would you like to continue?") # ...
```

None of these ideas is etched in stone. Feel free to call your input method prompt() or use a set of classes. Rework the interface any way you like.

The goal is to provide an easy-to-use yet robust method of requesting input. It should free the programmer of common concerns like calls to chomp() and ensuring valid input.

Quiz 8

Answer on page 125

Roman Numerals

This quiz asks you to write a converter to and from Roman numerals.

The script should be a standard Unix filter, reading from files specified on the command line or STDIN and writing to STDOUT. Each line of input will contain one integer (from 1 to 3,999[13]) expressed as an Arabic or Roman numeral. There should be one line of output for each line of input, containing the original number in the opposite format.

For example, given the following input:

```
III
29
38
CCXCI
1999
```

The correct output is as follows:

```
3
XXIX
XXXVIII
291
MCMXCIX
```

If you're not familiar with or need a refresher on Roman numerals, the rules are simple. First, seven letters are associated with seven values:

```
I = 1
V = 5
X = 10
L = 50
C = 100
D = 500
M = 1000
```

---

[13]Roman numerals for 4,000 and up do not use plain ASCII characters.

Second, you can combine letters to add values by listing them largest to smallest from left to right:

```
II     is 2
VIII   is 8
XXXI   is 31
```

However, you may list only three consecutive identical letters. That requires a special rule to express numbers like 40 and 900. That rule is that a single lower value may precede a larger value to indicate subtraction. This rule is used only to build values not reachable by the previous rules. Those numbers are as follows:

```
IV is 4
IX is 9
XL is 40
XC is 90
CD is 400
CM is 900
```

Quiz 9

Answer on page 135

Rock Paper Scissors

Generals, break out your copies of *The Art of War*[Tzu05], and let's get a little competition going!

Your task is to build some AI for playing the game Rock Paper Scissors against all manner of opponents. The challenge is to adapt to an opponent's strategy and seize the advantage...while he is doing the same to you, of course.

If you're not familiar with this childhood game, here's an overview: Two players choose one of three items at the same time: a rock, some paper, or scissors. The winner is determined by the following rules:

- Paper covers a rock. (Paper beats a rock.)
- Scissors cut paper. (Scissors beat paper.)
- A rock smashes scissors. (A rock beats scissors.)
- Anything else is a draw.

Defining a player is straightforward. I provide a class you can inherit from:

code/rock_paper_scissors/example_player.rb

```ruby
class YourPlayer < Player

  def initialize( opponent_name )
    # (optional) called at the start of a match verses opponent
    # opponent_name = String of opponent's class name
    #
    # Player's constructor sets @opponent_name
  end

  def choose
    # (required) return your choice of :paper, :rock or :scissors
  end
```

```ruby
  def result( your_choice, opponents_choice, win_lose_or_draw )
    # (optional) called after each choice you make to give feedback
    # your_choice      = your choice
    # oppenents_choice = opponent's choice
    # win_lose_or_draw = :win, :lose or :draw, your result
  end
end
```

We'll need some rules for defining players to make it easy for all our strategies to play against each other:

- Use one file for each strategy.

- A file should contain exactly one subclass of Player.

- Start the name of your subclass, the name of your files, and the name of any data files you write to disk with your initials.

Those rules should help with testing how different algorithms perform against each other.

Here are two dumb Players to practice with:

`code/rock_paper_scissors/jeg_paper_player.rb`

```ruby
#!/usr/biin/env ruby


class JEGPaperPlayer < Player
  def choose
    :paper
  end
end
```

`code/rock_paper_scissors/jeg_queue_player.rb`

```ruby
#!/usr/bin/env ruby


class JEGQueuePlayer < Player
  QUEUE = [ :rock, :scissors, :scissors ]

  def initialize( opponent_name )
    super
    @index = 0
  end

  def choose
    choice = QUEUE[@index]
    @index += 1
    @index = 0 if @index == QUEUE.size
    choice
  end
end
```

Here's how those two do against each other in a 1,000-game match (we will just track wins, since draws affect both players the same):

```
JEGPaperPlayer vs. JEGQueuePlayer
        JEGPaperPlayer: 334
        JEGQueuePlayer: 666
        JEGQueuePlayer Wins
```

Finally, here's the game engine that supports the players:

`code/rock_paper_scissors/rock_paper_scissors.rb`
```ruby
#!/usr/bin/env ruby

class Player
  @@players = [ ]

  def self.inherited( player )
    @@players << player
  end

  def self.each_pair
    (0...(@@players.size - 1)).each do |i|
      ((i + 1)...@@players.size).each do |j|
        yield @@players[i], @@players[j]
      end
    end
  end

  def initialize( opponent_name )
    @opponent_name = opponent_name
  end

  def choose
    raise NoMethodError, "Player subclasses must override choose()."
  end

  def result( your_choice, opponents_choice, win_lose_or_draw )
    # do nothing-subclasses can override as needed
  end
end

class Game
  def initialize( player1, player2 )
    @player1_name = player1.to_s
    @player2_name = player2.to_s
    @player1      = player1.new(@player2_name)
    @player2      = player2.new(@player1_name)

    @score1 = 0
    @score2 = 0
  end
```

```ruby
def play( num_matches )
  num_matches.times do
    hand1 = @player1.choose
    hand2 = @player2.choose

    [[@player1_name, hand1], [@player2_name, hand2]].each do |player, hand|
      unless [:rock, :paper, :scissors].include? hand
        raise "Invalid choice by #{player}."
      end
    end

    hands   = {hand1.to_s => @player1, hand2.to_s => @player2}
    choices = hands.keys.sort
    if choices.size == 1
      draw hand1, hand2
    elsif choices == %w{paper rock}
      win hands["paper"], hand1, hand2
    elsif choices == %w{rock scissors}
      win hands["rock"], hand1, hand2
    elsif choices == %w{paper scissors}
      win hands["scissors"], hand1, hand2
    end
  end
end

def results
  match = "#{@player1_name} vs. #{@player2_name}\n" +
          "\t#{@player1_name}: #{@score1}\n" +
          "\t#{@player2_name}: #{@score2}\n"
  if @score1 == @score2
    match + "\tDraw\n"
  elsif @score1 > @score2
    match + "\t#{@player1_name} Wins\n"
  else
    match + "\t#{@player2_name} Wins\n"
  end
end

private

def draw( hand1, hand2 )
  @score1 += 0.5
  @score2 += 0.5
  @player1.result(hand1, hand2, :draw)
  @player2.result(hand2, hand1, :draw)
end

def win( winner, hand1, hand2 )
  if winner == @player1
    @score1 += 1
    @player1.result(hand1, hand2, :win)
```

```
        @player2.result(hand2, hand1, :lose)
      else
        @score2 += 1
        @player1.result(hand1, hand2, :lose)
        @player2.result(hand2, hand1, :win)
      end
    end
  end
end

match_game_count = 1000
if ARGV.size > 2 and ARGV[0] == "-m" and ARGV[1] =~ /^[1-9]\d*$/
  ARGV.shift
  match_game_count = ARGV.shift.to_i
end

ARGV.each do |p|
  if test(?d, p)
    Dir.foreach(p) do |file|
      next if file =~ /^\./
      next unless file =~ /\.rb$/
      require File.join(p, file)
    end
  else
    require p
  end
end

Player.each_pair do |one, two|
  game = Game.new one, two
  game.play match_game_count
  puts game.results
end
```

You can use the engine with a command like the following:

```
$ rock_paper_scissors.rb jeg_paper_player.rb jeg_queue_player.rb
```

Or you can point it at a directory, and it will treat all the .rb files in there as Players:

```
$ rock_paper_scissors.rb players/
```

You can also change the match game count:

```
$ rock_paper_scissors.rb -m 10000 players/
```

Quiz 10
Answer on page 141

Knight's Travails

Posed by J E Bailey

Given a standard 8×8 chessboard where each position is indicated in algebraic notation (with the lower-left corner being a1), design a script that accepts two or more arguments.

The first argument indicates the starting position of a standard chess knight. The second argument indicates the ending position of the knight. Any additional arguments indicate positions that are forbidden.

Return an array indicating the shortest path that the knight must travel to get to the end position without landing on one of the forbidden squares. If there is no valid path to the destination, return **nil**.

Knights move in an L-shaped pattern. They may move two squares in any of the four cardinal directions and then turn 90 degrees and move an additional square. So a knight on e4 can jump to d2, f2, c3, g3, c5, g5, d6, or f6:

```
$ knights_travails a8 b7 b6
["c7", "b5", "d6", "b7"]

$ knights_travails a8 g6 b6 c7
nil
```

If you're not familiar with algebraic chess notation, Figure 1.1, on the following page, shows the name of every square on the board.

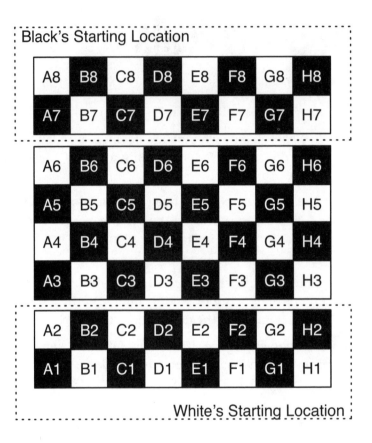

Figure 1.1: Chess Squares by Name

Quiz 11
Answer on page 149

Sokoban

Ruby isn't the only good thing to come out of Japan. The computer game Sokoban, invented by Hiroyuki Imabayashi, was introduced by Thinking Rabbit in 1982. This game of logic puzzles was an instant success. It won awards and spawned sequels. Over the years, Sokoban has been ported to a huge number of platforms. Fan support remains strong, and many of those fans still produce new levels for the game.

This quiz is to implement the game of Sokoban with the interface of your choosing and any extra features you would like to have.

Sokoban (which translates to *Warehouse Man*) has simple rules, which basically amount to this: push crates into their storage spots in the warehouse.

The elements of the levels are simple: there's a man, some crates and walls, open floor, and storage. Different level designers use various characters to represent these items in level data files. Here's one possible set of symbols:

@	for the man	o	for crates
#	for walls	*a space*	for open floor
.	for storage		

Now because a man or a crate can also be on a storage space, we need special conditions to represent those setups:

*	for a crate on storage
+	for a man on storage

Using this, we can build an extremely simple level:

```
#####
#.o@#
#####
```

This level is completely surrounded by walls, as all Sokoban levels must be. Walls are, of course, impassable. In the center we have from left to right: a storage space, a crate (on open floor), and the man (also on open floor).

The game is played by moving the man up, down, left and right. When the man moves toward a crate, he may push it along in front of him as long as there is no wall or second crate behind the one being pushed. A level is solved when all crates are on storage spaces.

Given those rules, we can solve our level with a single move to the left, yielding the following:

```
#####
#*@ #
#####
```

That simple system can lead to some surprisingly complicated mind benders, but please don't take my word for it. Build the game, and see for yourself.[14] Be warned, Sokoban is extremely addictive!

---

[14]You can find some premade levels to test your game engine and your logic skills at http://www.rubyquiz.com/sokoban_levels.txt. These levels are copyrighted by Thinking Rabbit.

Quiz
Answer on page 161

12

Crosswords

For this quiz let's tackle a classic problem. I've seen it just about everywhere in some form or another, but I believe Donald E. Knuth may have first made it a popular challenge.

The quiz is to lay out crossword puzzles. A puzzle layout will be provided in a file, with the file name passed as a command-line argument. The layout will be formatted as such:

```
X _ _ _ _ X X
_ _ X _ _ _ _
_ _ _ _ X _ _
_ X _ _ X X X
_ _ _ X _ _ _
X _ _ _ _ _ X
```

Xs denote filled-in squares, and underscores are where a puzzle worker would enter letters. Each row of the puzzle is on a new line. The spaces are a readability tool and should be ignored by your program. In the final layout, squares should look like this:

```
######  Filled-in square
######
######
######

######  Letter square
#    #
#    #
######
```

Now, when we combine these squares, we don't want to double up on borders, so this:

```
_ _
X _
```

should become the following:

```
##########
#    #    #
#    #    #
##########
#####    #
#####    #
##########
```

As a style point, many crosswords drop filled squares on the outer
edges. We wouldn't want our Ruby-generated crosswords to be unfash-
ionable, so we better do that too:

```
X _ X          would render as:          #####
_ _ _                                     #   #
                                          #   #
                                  ###############
                                  #   #   #   #
                                  #   #   #   #
                                  ###############
```

The final step of laying out a crossword puzzle is to number the squares
for word placement. A square is numbered if it is the first square in a
word going left to right or top to bottom. A word must be at least two
letters long, so don't number individual squares. Numbers start at 1
and count up left to right, row by row going down.

Putting all that together, here is a sample layout. (This was generated
from the layout format at the beginning of this quiz.)

```
      ####################
      #1   #    #2   #3   #
      #    #    #    #    #    #
#################################
#4   #    #####5   #    #6   #7   #
#    #    #####    #    #    #    #
#################################
#8   #    #9   #    #    #10  #    #
#    #    #    #    #    #    #    #
####################    ##########
#    ######11  #    #
#    #####    #    #
#################################
#12  #13  #    ######14  #15  #    #
#    #    #    #####    #    #    #
#################################
      #16  #    #    #    #    #
      #    #    #    #    #    #
      #######################
```

Solutions should output (only) the finished crossword to STDOUT.

Quiz 13
Answer on page 169

1-800-THE-QUIZ

Companies like to list their phone numbers using the letters printed on telephones. This makes the number easier to remember for customers. A famous example is 1-800-PICK-UPS.

This quiz is to write a program that shows the user possible matches for a list of provided phone numbers. For example, if your program is fed the following number:

```
873.7829
```

one possible line of output (according to my dictionary) is this:

```
USE-RUBY
```

Your script should behave as a standard Unix filter, reading from files specified as command-line arguments or STDIN when no files are given. Each line of these files will contain a single phone number, seven digits in length.

For each phone number read, output all possible word replacements from a dictionary. Your script should try to replace every digit of the provided phone number with a letter from a dictionary word; however, if no match can be made, a single digit can be left between two words. No two consecutive digits can remain unchanged, and the program should skip over a number (producing no output) if a match cannot be made.

Your solution should allow the user to select a dictionary with the -d command-line option, but it's fine to use a reasonable default for your system. The dictionary is expected to have one word per line.

All punctuation and whitespace should be ignored in both phone numbers and the dictionary file. The program should not be case sensitive, letting "a" == "A". Output should be capital letters, and digits should be separated at word boundaries with a single hyphen (-), one possible encoding per line.

The number encoding on my phone is as follows:

```
2 = A B C
3 = D E F
4 = G H I
5 = J K L
6 = M N O
7 = P Q R S
8 = T U V
9 = W X Y Z
```

Feel free to use that or the encoding on your own phone.

Quiz 14
Answer on page 177

Texas Hold'em

Posed by Matthew D Moss

For this Ruby Quiz, let's identify and rank poker hands. Say we have the following sample game of the popular Texas hold'em, where you try to make the best five-card hand from a total of seven cards (five shared among all players):

```
Kc 9s Ks Kd 9d 3c 6d
9c Ah Ks Kd 9d 3c 6d
Ac Qc Ks Kd 9d 3c
9h 5s
4d 2d Ks Kd 9d 3c 6d
7s Ts Ks Kd 9d
```

Each line represents a player's final hand. The cards of the hand are separated by a space. The first character is the face value of the card, and the second is the suit. Cards have one of four suits: clubs, diamonds, hearts, or spades. Cards also have a face value that is one of (from highest to lowest) the following: ace, king, queen, jack, ten, nine, eight, seven, six, five, four, three, or two. The ace is almost always high, but watch for the exceptions in the hands.

Some players didn't make it to seven cards, because they folded before the end of the game, and we can ignore those hands. For the rest, we want to declare the hand they ended up with and indicate a winner, or winners in the event of a tie. We should also rearrange named hands so the five used cards are at the front of the listing. That gives us the following for our sample hand:

```
Kd Ks Kc 9d 9s 6d 3c Full House (Winner)
Ks Kd 9d 9c Ah 6d 3c Two Pair
Ac Qc Ks Kd 9d 3c
9h 5s
Kd 9d 6d 4d 2d Ks 3c Flush
7s Ts Ks Kd 9d
```

Let's cover the poker hands as a refresher for anyone who doesn't have them memorized or has never seen them. The following listing is from best hand to worst:

Royal flush:

This coveted poker hand is easy to spot. A person must have the ace, king, queen, jack, and ten of a single suit. It can be any of the four suits, but all five cards must share it.

Straight flush:

A straight flush is similar to the royal flush, save that the face value of the cards can be anything, as long as they go in order. Again, the suits must match. In a straight flush, the ace is allowed to be the highest card (above the king) or the lowest (below the two).

Four of a kind:

Just as the name suggests, this hand is four of any face value.

Full house:

Three of any face value and two of another.

Flush:

Five cards of the same suit. Face value doesn't matter.

Straight:

Just like the straight flush, except the suit doesn't need to match. Remember that the ace can be high or low here.

Three of a kind:

Three of any one face value.

Two pair:

Two cards of one face value and two of another.

Pair:

Two cards with the same face value.

High card:

When you have nothing better, your hand is valued by the highest card in the hand. We might say you have "jack high," for example.

You really don't need to know any more details of Texas hold'em for this quiz, save for how to break a tie. First, not all hands are created equal, even if they have the same name. The higher set of cards always wins. So a flush, king high, beats a flush, queen high, and a pair of threes is better than a pair of twos.

If the hands are still a tie, kickers come into play. If the hand doesn't use all five cards, the remaining cards, or *kickers* as they are called, are compared one at a time to see whether one player has a higher card. Remember that you can use only your five best cards to make a hand, though. Two are ignored completely.

Here's a script by Matthew D Moss for generating test games:

```
code/texas_holdem/game_gen.rb
FACES = "AKQJT98765432"
SUITS = "cdhs"

deck = []                          # build a deck
FACES.each_byte do |f|
  SUITS.each_byte do |s|
    deck.push(f.chr + s.chr)
  end
end

3.times do                         # shuffle deck
  shuf = []
  deck.each do |c|
    loc = rand(shuf.size + 1)
    shuf.insert(loc, c)
  end
  deck = shuf.reverse
end

common = Array.new(5) { deck.pop }   # deal common cards

# deal player's hole cards
hole = Array.new(8) { Array.new(2) { deck.pop } }

hands = []                         # output hands
all_fold = true
while all_fold do
  hands = []
  hole.each do |h|
    num_common = [0, 3, 4, 5][rand(4)]
    if num_common == 5
      all_fold = false
    end
    if num_common > 0
      hand = h + common[0 ... num_common]
    else
      hand = h
    end
    hands.push(hand.join(' '))
  end
end

hands.each { |h| puts h }
```

Quiz **15**
Answer on page 183

Solitaire Cipher

Cryptologist Bruce Schneier designed the hand cipher Solitaire[15] for Neal Stephenson's book *Cryptonomicon*[Ste00]. Created to be the first truly secure hand cipher, Solitaire requires only a deck of cards for the encryption and decryption of messages.

While it's true that Solitaire is easily completed by hand, using a computer is much quicker and easier. Because of that, Solitaire conversion routines are available in many programming languages.

The quiz is to write a Ruby script that does the encryption and decryption of messages using the Solitaire cipher.

Encryption

Let's look at the steps of encrypting a message with Solitaire:

1. Discard any non–A to Z characters, and uppercase all remaining letters. Split the message into five character groups, using Xs to pad the last group, if needed. If we begin with the message "Code in Ruby, live longer!" for example, we would now have:

   CODEI NRUBY LIVEL ONGER

2. Use Solitaire to generate a keystream letter for each letter in the message. This step is detailed in Section I, *The Keystream*, on page 43, but for the sake of example, let's just say we get this:

   DWJXH YRFDG TMSHP UURXJ

3. Convert the message from step 1 into numbers, A = 1, B = 2, and so on:

   3 15 4 5 9   14 18 21 2 25   12 9 22 5 12   15 14 7 5 18

---

[15]The official site for Solitaire is at http://www.schneier.com/solitaire.html.

4. Convert the keystream letters from step 2 using the same method:

```
4 23 10 24 8    25 18 6 4 7    20 13 19 8 16    21 21 18 24 10
```

5. Add the message numbers from step 3 to the keystream numbers from step 4 and subtract 26 from the result if it is greater than 26. For example, 6 + 10 = 16 as expected, but 26 + 1 = 1 (27 - 26):

```
7 12 14 3 17    13 10 1 6 6    6 22 15 13 2    10 9 25 3 2
```

6. Convert the numbers from step 5 back to letters:

```
GLNCQ MJAFF FVOMB JIYCB
```

At this point, we have our hidden message. Now we just need to be able to reverse the process.

Decryption

Decrypting with Solitaire is even easier, so let's look at those steps now. We'll work backward with our example now, decrypting GLNCQ MJAFF FVOMB JIYCB:

1. Use Solitaire to generate a keystream letter for each letter in the message to be decoded. Again, I detail this process shortly, but the sender and receiver use the same key and will get the same letters:

```
DWJXH YRFDG TMSHP UURXJ
```

2. Convert the message to be decoded to numbers:

```
7 12 14 3 17    13 10 1 6 6    6 22 15 13 2    10 9 25 3 2
```

3. Convert the keystream letters from step 1 to numbers:

```
4 23 10 24 8    25 18 6 4 7    20 13 19 8 16    21 21 18 24 10
```

4. Subtract the keystream numbers from step 3 from the message numbers from step 2. If the keystream number is less than or equal to the message number, add 26 to the keystream number before subtracting. For example, 22 - 1 = 21 as expected, but 1 - 22 = 5 (27 - 22):

```
3 15 4 5 9    14 18 21 2 25    12 9 22 5 12    15 14 7 5 18
```

5. Convert the numbers from step 4 back to letters:

```
CODEI NRUBY LIVEL ONGER
```

That's all there is to transforming messages. Finally, let's look at the missing piece of the puzzle, generating the keystream letters.

The Keystream

First, let's talk a little about the deck of cards. Solitaire needs a full deck of 52 cards and the two jokers. The jokers need to be visually distinct. I'll refer to them here as A and B.

Some steps involve assigning a value to the cards. In those cases, use the cards face value as a base, ace is 1, two is 2, ... ten is 10, jack is 11, queen is 12, and king is 13. Then modify the base by the bridge ordering of suits. Clubs is just the base value, diamonds is the base value + 13, hearts is the base value + 26, and spades is base value + 39. Either joker has a value of 53.

When the cards must represent a letter, club and diamond values are taken to be the number of the letter (1 to 26), as are heart and spade values after subtracting 26 from their value (27 to 52 drops to 1 to 26). Jokers are never used as letters. Now let's make sense of all that by putting it to use:

1. Key the deck. This is the critical step in the actual operation of the cipher and the heart of its security. There are many methods to go about this, such as shuffling a deck and then arranging the receiving deck in the same order or tracking a bridge column in the paper and using that to order the cards.

   Because we want to be able to test our answers, though, we'll use an unkeyed deck, cards in order of value. That is, from top to bottom, we'll always start with the following deck:

   ```
   Ace of clubs
   ...to...
   King of clubs
   Ace of diamonds
   ...to...
   King of diamonds
   Ace of hearts
   ...to...
   King of hearts
   Ace of spades
   ...to...
   King of spades
   "A" joker
   "B" joker
   ```

2. Move the A joker down one card. If the joker is at the bottom of the deck, move it to just below the first card. (Consider the deck

to be circular.) The first time we do this with an unkeyed deck, it will go from this:

```
1 2 3 ... 52 A B
```

to this:

```
1 2 3 ... 52 B A
```

3. Move the B joker down two cards. If the joker is the bottom card, move it just below the second card. If the joker is the just above the bottom card, move it below the top card. (Again, consider the deck to be circular.) This changes our example deck to the following:

```
1 B 2 3 4 ... 52 A
```

4. Perform a triple cut around the two jokers—that is, split the deck into three chunks around the two cards, and then swap the top and bottom chunk. All cards above the top joker move to below the bottom joker, and vice versa. The jokers and the cards between them do not move. This gives us the following:

```
B 2 3 4 ... 52 A 1
```

5. Perform a count cut using the value of the bottom card. Count the bottom card's value in cards off the top of the deck, and move them just above the bottom card. This changes our deck to the following:

```
2 3 4 ... 52 A B 1   (the 1 tells us to move just the B)
```

6. Find the output letter. Convert the top card to its value, and count down that many cards from the top of the deck, with the top card itself being card 1. Look at the card immediately after your count, and convert it to a letter. This is the next letter in the keystream. If the output card is a joker, no letter is generated this sequence. This step does not alter the deck. For our example, the output letter is as follows:

```
D   (the 2 tells us to count down to the 4, which is a D)
```

7. Return to step 2, if more letters are needed.

For the sake of testing, the first ten output letters for an unkeyed deck are as follows:

```
D (4)
W (49)
J (10)
```

```
Skip Joker (53)
X (24)
H (8)
Y (51)
R (44)
F (6)
D (4)
G (33)
```

That's all there is to Solitaire. It's really longer to explain than it is to code.

Your Script

Solutions to this quiz should accept a message as a command-line argument and encrypt or decrypt it as needed. It should be easy to tell which is needed by the pattern of the message, but you can use a switch if you prefer.

All the examples for this quiz assume an unkeyed deck, but your script can provide a way to key the deck, if desired. (A real script would require this, of course.)

Here are a couple of messages to test your work with. You'll know when you have them right:

```
CLEPK HHNIY CFPWH FDFEH
```

```
ABVAW LWZSY OORYK DUPVH
```

Quiz **16**
Answer on page 193

English Numerals

Posed by Timothy Byrd

While we normally write numbers using Arabic numerals, numbers can also be written out as English phrases.

For example:

```
7    == seven
42   == forty-two
2001 == two thousand and one
1999 == one thousand nine hundred and ninety-nine
```

Given that, this quiz is a problem from a Pi Mu Epsilon newsletter:[16]

> *When the integers 1 to 10,000,000,000 are written in the English language and then sorted as strings, which odd number appears first in the list?*

Your task is to do the following:

- Create Ruby code to translate a number to its English-language form. (My sample version works with integers less than 10^{72}.)

- Write a program to determine which *odd* number in between 1 and 10,000,000,000 would sort first if written in English. (Brute force is the obvious solution, but the computer may have to think about the answer....)

---

[16]The U.S. national math club, http://www.pme-math.org/

Quiz 17

Answer on page 201

Code Cleaning

I'm always very vocal about how Ruby Quiz isn't interested in golf[17] and obfuscation.[18] It's my own private fight for clean code.

To be fair, though, you can really learn a lot from practices such as golf and obfuscation. It will teach you a surprising number of details about the inner workings of your language of choice.

Here's my compromise.

This challenge is to utterly clean some famous examples of compressed Ruby code. Refactor the code until it's as readable as possible, whatever that means to you.

For those who faint at the sight of dense code, I offer an "easier" challenge. Try this code by Mauricio Fernández:

`code/code_cleaning/wiki.cgi`
```
#!/usr/bin/ruby -rcgi
H,B=%w' HomePage w7.cgi?n=%s' ;c=CGI.new' html4' ;n,d=c['n' ]!='' ?c['n' ]:H,c['d' ];t='
cat #{n}';d!='' &&'echo #{t=CGI.escapeHTML(d)} >#{n}';c.instance_eval{out{h1{n}+
a(B%H){H}+pre{t.gsub(/([A-Z]\w+){2}/){a(B%$&){$&}}}+form("get"){textarea('d'){t
}+hidden('n' ,n)+submit}}}
```

If you prefer a "trickier" challenge, I offer this famous code from Florian Groß. Just take a deep breath before turning the page....

---

[17]Writing code with as few keystrokes as possible
[18]An intentional effort to make code difficult to read

```
code/code_cleaning/p2p.rb
#!/usr/bin/ruby
# Server: ruby p2p.rb password server public-uri private-uri merge-servers
# Sample: ruby p2p.rb foobar server druby://123.123.123.123:1337
#         druby://:1337 druby://foo.bar:1337
# Client: ruby p2p.rb password client server-uri download-pattern [list-only]
# Sample: ruby p2p.rb foobar client druby://localhost:1337 *.rb
################################################################
# You are not allowed to use this application for anything illegal
# unless you live in a sane place. Insane places currently include
# California (see link) and might soon include the complete
# USA. People using this software are responsible for themselves. I
# can't prevent them from doing illegal stuff for obvious reasons. So
# have fun and do whatever you can get away with for now.
#
# http://info.sen.ca.gov/pub/bill/sen/sb_0051-0100/
#      sb_96_bill_20050114_introduced.html
################################################################
require' drb' ;F=File;def c(u)DRbObject.new((),u)end;def x(u)[P,u].hash;end;def s(
p)F.basename p[/[^|]+/]end;P,M,U,V,*O=$*;M["s"]?(DRb.start_service V,Class.new{
def p(z=0)O.push(*z).uniq;end;new.methods.map{|m|m[/_[_t]/]||private(m)};def y;(
p(U)+p).map{|u|u!=U&&c(u).f(x(u),p(U))};self;end;def f(c,a=0,t=2)x(U)==c&&t<1?
Dir[s(a)]:t<2?[*open(s(a),"rb")]:p(a)end}.new.y;sleep):c(U).f(x(U)).map{|n|c(n).
f(x(n),V,0).map{|f|s f}.map{|f|O[0]?p(f):open(f,"wb")<<c(n).f(x(n),f,1)}}
```

This is a little different from a traditional Ruby Quiz, but I encourage
all to play and learn. I promise to return to normal challenges in the
next chapter.

Answer on page 209

Quiz 18

Banned Words

Posed by Fredrik Jagenheim

At work, we discovered that they installed a spam filter that throws away email that it considers to be spam. Rather than using a Bayesian filter where words contribute to a probability that the message is spam, it simply checks for certain words that it considers *banned*. One word we discovered was *sex*, which is a Swedish word for the number six. So the Swedish translation of the phrase "I'll be home at six o'clock" will be classified as spam, thrown away and never seen.

The Ruby Quiz I propose is to figure out which words are banned. Since the filter is a black box, we can find out which words are banned only by sending email through it. The real problem is to find out how to do it with as *few* emails as possible.

Of course, I don't want the Ruby community to do a denial-of-service attack on my employer's mail server, so do it as a local filter. Perhaps try something like this:

`code/banned_words/filter.rb`

```ruby
# A filter class for managing a given _banned_words_ list.
class LanguageFilter

  # Create a new LanguageFilter object that will
  # disallow _banned_words_.
  #
  # Accepts a list of words, arrays of words,
  # or a combination of the two.

  def initialize( *banned_words )
    @banned_words = banned_words.flatten.sort
    @clean_calls = 0
  end

  # A count of the calls to <i>clean?</i>.
```

```
attr_reader :clean_calls

# Test if provided _text_ is allowable by this filter.
#
# Returns *false* if _text_ contains _banned_words_,
# *true* if it does not.

def clean?( text )
  @clean_calls += 1
  @banned_words.each do |word|
    return false if text =~ /\b#{word}\b/
  end
  true
end

# Verify a _suspect_words_ list against the actual
# _banned_words_ list.
#
# Returns *false* if the two lists are not identical or
# *true* if the lists do match.
#
# Accepts a list of words, arrays of words,
# or a combination of the two.

def verify( *suspect_words )
  suspect_words.flatten.sort == @banned_words
end
end

filter = LanguageFilter.new "six"

filter.clean?("I'll be home at six.")             # => false
filter.clean?("Do not taunt the happy fun ball!") # => true

filter.verify("ball") # => false
filter.verify("six")  # => true

filter.clean_calls # => 2
```

Figure out how to find the hidden words using as few calls to Language-Filter.clean?() as possible.

Which algorithms are effective when many words are blocked (say 10%), and which are effective when very few are blocked (1 in 20,000)?

All solutions should do better than this:

```
dict = ["foo", "bar", "six", "baz"]
filter = LanguageFilter.new "six"

puts dict.reject { |word| filter.clean?(word) }
```

Quiz 19
Answer on page 213

Secret Santas

Honoring a long-standing (and fun) tradition started by my wife's father, my friends play a Secret Santa game each year around Christmas time.

If you're not familiar with how a Secret Santa game is played, you really are missing out on some fun. All players write their names on small pieces of paper that are folded up, placed in a hat, and mixed well. Each player then secretly draws a name in turn. Often the draw will have to be repeated a couple of times, until no players draw their own names. Santas then spend days surprising the person they drew with gifts and clues to Santa's identity. This is a fun way to spread holiday cheer.

Unfortunately, the hat draw can be tedious. The system is prone to "Wait, I got myself..." problems, which can require several draws.

This year, my friends added a rule that further complicated the draw. Since we're no good at hiding suspicious behavior from our spouses, we now prevent family members from drawing each other. This makes it harder to guess who has who. Unfortunately, we knew the hat would not stand up to the challenge.

The quiz is to replace our hat with a Secret Santa–choosing script.

Your script should accept a list of names on STDIN. Each line will contain a first name and a family name, separated by a space:

`code/secret_santa/testdata`

```
Mr. Gray
Mrs. Gray
Mr. Thomas
Mrs. Thomas
Mr. Matsumoto
Mrs. Matsumoto
Mr. Fulton
```

We'll keep things simple and say that people have only two names, so you don't have to worry about tricky names like Gray II.

Your script must choose a Secret Santa for every name in the list. Players cannot be assigned their own names or anyone else with the same family name.

Your script should output a list of player names. Alongside each name it will show another name—the person receiving that player's gifts. Thus the following:

```
Mr. Thomas -> Mr. Gray
```

would indicate that Mr. Thomas is giving gifts to Mr. Gray.

Quiz 20
Answer on page 221

Barrel of Monkeys

Posed by Gavin Kistner

Last week one of the local radio stations was having a "Barrel of Monkeys" afternoon. While a song was playing, listeners would call in and suggest the next song, which had to begin with the same letter as the playing song ended in.

So, for example, a sample (eclectic) Barrel of Monkeys playlist might be as follows:

1. "Peace Train"
2. "No More 'I Love You's'"
3. "Super Trooper"
4. "Rock Me, Amadeus"
5. "Song of the South"
6. "Hooked on a Feeling"
7. "Go Tell It on the Mountain"

See how each song name begins with the last letter of the name of the song before it?

Just creating any playlist would be too easy, however. We need a worthy problem to solve:

1. Given any starting and ending song, create a playlist that connects the two songs.

2. For extra credit, try to create a playlist of a specific duration (to fill a particular time slot on the radio).

3. For more extra credit, try to find the shortest playlist that links the songs (either in terms of number of songs or total play time).

You can find an XML file with more than 5,000 song names and play times at http://rubyquiz.com/SongLibrary.xml.gz (100KB compressed). The song durations are in milliseconds.

Finally, because this problem may be enough fun without having to discover trouble yourself, I offer a few things to think about here:

- What do you do with songs with names like "'74-'75" or "Seventy Times 7" or "=:0 :("?

- How about a song named "Candy Everybody Wants (unplugged)" or "Voulez-Vous [Extended Remix, 1979 US Promo]" or "Speed Racer - Hardcore Mix" or "Breathe Remix Feat Sean Paul"?

- What do you do if there is no way to connect two songs? (And how do you know for sure?)

Quiz 21
Answer on page 233

Amazing Mazes

Posed by Matthew Linnell

Why don't we try our hand at mazes? We can define the two basic components of this problem as follows:

- Generating the maze
- Solving the maze

Generating the Maze

The maze is to be rectangular in shape, with the height and width determined at run time. Each node of the maze is a square area surrounded by walls on up to three sides.

All nodes of the maze must be reachable from any point. In other words, if one were to randomly pick a starting point and destination, the maze is always solvable. Furthermore, let us enforce that only one viable solution for the maze exists for any given starting point and destination (you cannot reach the same destination using two different routes).

Your first task is to generate ASCII output representing the maze. Figure 1.2, on the following page, shows a sample 10×10 maze.

Solving the Maze

Given a maze produced from your previous code, find the solution. Produce ASCII output to demonstrate the solution.

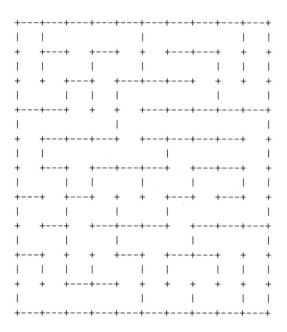

Figure 1.2: Sample 10×10 maze

Bonus Points

Here are some bonus tasks:

1. Calculate which starting point and destination in the maze give you the longest possible path.

2. Calculate which starting point and destination give the most complicated path (involve the most turns).

Here is an example command-line execution:

```
$ ruby maze.rb {height} {width} [ {start} {stop} ]
```

Quiz
Answer on page 245

22

Learning Tic-Tac-Toe

This Ruby Quiz is to implement some AI for playing tic-tac-toe, with a catch: you're not allowed to embed any knowledge of the game into your creation beyond making legal moves and recognizing that it has won or lost.

Your program is expected to "learn" from the games it plays, until it masters the game and can play flawlessly.

Tic-tac-toe is a very easy game played on a 3×3 board like this:

```
   |   |
---+---+---
   |   |
---+---+---
   |   |
```

Two players take turns filling a single open square with their symbol. The first person to play uses *X*s, and the other player uses *O*s. The first player to get a run of three symbols across, down, or diagonally wins. If the board fills without a run, the game is a draw. Here's what a game won by the *X* player might end up looking like:

```
   |   | X
---+---+---
   | X |
---+---+---
 X | O | O
```

Submissions can have any interface but should be able to play against humans interactively. However, I also suggest making it easy to play against another AI player so you can "teach" the program faster.

Being able to monitor the learning progression and know when a program has mastered the game would be very interesting, if you can find a way to incorporate it into your solution.

Quiz **23**
Answer on page 259

Countdown

Posed by Brian Candler

One of the longest-running quiz shows on British television is called *Countdown*. That show has a "numbers round." Some cards are laid face down in front of the host. The top row contains *large* numbers (from the set 25, 50, 75, and 100), and the rest are *small* (1 to 10). Numbers are duplicated in the cards. Six cards are picked and displayed: the choice is made by one of the contestants, who typically will ask for one large number and five small ones.

Next, a machine called Cecil picks a target number from 100 to 999 at random. The contestants then have 30 seconds to find a way of combining the source numbers using the normal arithmetic operators (+, -, *, and /) to make the target number or to get as close as possible.

Each source card can be used just once. The same applies to any intermediate results (although of course you don't have to explicitly show the intermediate results).

For example, if the target number is 522 and the source cards are 100, 5, 5, 2, 6, and 8, a possible solution is as follows:

```
100 *   5 = 500
  5 +   6 =  11
 11 *   2 =  22
500 +  22 = 522
```

or more succinctly, (5 * 100) + ((5 + 6) * 2) = 522. Another solution is (100 + 6) * 5 - 8 = 522.

Normal arithmetic rules apply. Each step of the calculation must result in an integer value.

The quiz is to write a program that will accept one target number and a list of source numbers and generate a solution that calculates the target or a number as close to the target as possible.

Quiz 24

Answer on page 269

Solving Tactics

Posed by Bob Sidebotham

There is a pencil and paper game, Tactics, played on a 4×4 grid. The play starts with an empty grid. On each turn, a player can fill in from one to four adjacent squares, either horizontally or vertically. The player who fills in the last square loses.

Here's a sample game to help clarify the previous rules. The board position at the end of each play is shown:

```
First player    Second player

X X X X         X X X X        (Turn 1)
_ _ _ _         _ _ _ _
_ _ _ _         _ _ X _
_ _ _ _         _ _ X _

X X X X         X X X X        (Turn 2)
X X _ _         X X _ X
_ _ X _         _ _ X X
_ _ X _         _ _ X _

X X X X         X X X X        (Turn 3)
X X _ X         X X X X
_ _ X X         _ _ X X
_ _ X X         _ _ X X

X X X X         X X X X        (Turn 4)
X X X X         X X X X
X X X X         X X X X
_ _ X X         X _ X X

X X X X                        (Turn 5
X X X X                         Second
X X X X                         player
X X X X                         wins!)
```

Your task is to write a Ruby program that, given only these rules, determines whether the first or second player is bound to be the winner, assuming perfect play. It should do this in a "reasonable" amount of time and memory—it should definitely take less than a minute on any processor less than five years old. You get bonus points if you can make the case that your program actually gets the right answer for the right reason!

Quiz **25**

Answer on page 279

Cryptograms

Posed by Glenn P. Parker

Given a cryptogram and a dictionary of known words, find the best possible solution(s) to the cryptogram. You get extra points for speed. Coding a brute-force solution is relatively easy, but there are many opportunities for the clever optimizer.

A *cryptogram* is piece of text that has been passed through a simple cipher that maps all instances of one letter to a different letter. The familiar rot13[19] encoding is a trivial example.

A solution to a cryptogram is a one-to-one mapping between two sets of (up to) 26 letters, such that applying the map to the cryptogram yields the greatest possible number of words in the dictionary.

Both the dictionary and the cryptogram are presented as a set of words, one per line. The script should output one or more solutions and the full or partial mapping for each solution. A cryptogram might be as follows:

```
gebo
tev
e
cwaack
cegn
gsatkb
ussyk
```

Its solution could be as follows:

```
mary
had
```

---

[19]An encoding where the first 13 letters of the alphabet are swapped with the last 13, and vice versa. In Ruby that's just some_string.tr("A-Za-z", "N-ZA-Mn-za-m").

```
a
little
lamb
mother
goose
```

This is solved using the following mapping:

```
in:  abcdefghijklmnopqrstuvwxyz
out: trl.a.m...e..by...ohgdi.s.
```

(The dots in the "out" side of the mapping indicate unused input letters.)

Three unsolved cryptograms are given. Each cryptogram uses a different mapping. The cryptograms may contain a few words that are not in the dictionary (for example, an author's name is commonly appended to quoted text in cryptograms). Many published cryptograms also contain punctuation in plain text as a clue to the solver. The following cryptograms contain no punctuation, since it just confuses dictionary-based searches:

```
code/cryptograms/crypto1.txt
zfsbhd
bd
lsf
xfe
ofsr
bsdxbejrbls
sbsfra
sbsf
xfe
ofsr
xfedxbejrbls
rqlujd
jvwj
fpbdls
```

```
code/cryptograms/crypto2.txt
mkr
ideerqruhr
nrmsrru
mkr
ozgcym
qdakm
scqi
oui
mkr
qdakm
scqi
dy
mkr
```

```
ideerqruhr
nrmsrru
mkr
zdakmudua
nja
oui
mkr
zdakmudua
goqb
msodu
```

`code/cryptograms/crypto3.txt`

```
ftyw
uwmb
yw
ilwwv
qvb
bjtvi
fupxiu
t
dqvi
tv
yj
huqtvd
mtrw
fuw
dwq
bjmqv
fupyqd
```

The dictionary I used was2of4brif.txt, available as part of the 12Dicts
package at http://prdownloads.sourceforge.net/wordlist/12dicts-4.0.zip.

Part II

Answers and Discussion

Mad Libs

These are a fun little distraction, eh? Actually, I was surprised to discover (when writing the quiz) how practical this challenge is. Mad Libs are really just a templating problem, and that comes up in many aspects of programming. Have a look at the "views" in Ruby on Rails[20] for a strong real-world example.

Looking at the problem that way got me to thinking, doesn't Ruby ship with a templating engine? Yes, it does.

Ruby includes a standard library called ERB.[21] ERB allows you to embed Ruby code into any text document. When that text is run through the library, the embedded code is run. This can be used to dynamically build up document content.

For this example, we need only one feature of ERB. When we run ERB on a file, any Ruby code inside of the funny-looking <%= ... %> tags will be executed, and the value returned by that execution code will be inserted into the document. Think of this as delayed interpolation (like Ruby's #{ ... }, but it happens when triggered instead of when a String is built).[22]

Let's put ERB to work:

`code/madlibs/erb_madlib.rb`
```
#!/usr/local/bin/ruby -w

# use Ruby's standard template engine
require "erb"
```

---

[20]Ruby on Rails, or just *Rails* to those who know it well, is a popular web application framework written in Ruby. You can learn more at http://www.rubyonrails.org/.

[21]ERB is eRuby's pure-Ruby cousin. eRuby is written in C and stands for "embedded Ruby."

[22]You can learn about ERB's other features from the online documentation at http://www.ruby-doc.org/stdlib/libdoc/erb/rdoc/index.html.

```ruby
# storage for keyed question reuse
$answers = Hash.new

# asks a madlib question and returns an answer
def q_to_a( question )
  question.gsub!(/\s+/, " ")          # normalize spacing

  if $answers.include? question       # keyed question
    $answers[question]
  else                                # new question
    key = if question.sub!(/^\s*(.+?)\s*:\s*/, "") then $1 else nil end

    print "Give me #{question}:   "
    answer = $stdin.gets.chomp

    $answers[key] = answer unless key.nil?

    answer
  end
end

# usage
unless ARGV.size == 1 and test(?e, ARGV[0])
  puts "Usage:  #{File.basename($PROGRAM_NAME)} MADLIB_FILE"
  exit
end

# load Madlib, with title
madlib = "\n#{File.basename(ARGV.first, '.madlib').tr('_', ' ')}\n\n" +
         File.read(ARGV.first)
# convert ((...)) to <%= q_to_a('...') %>
madlib.gsub!(/\(\(\(\s*(.+?)\s*\)\)/, "<%= q_to_a(' \\1') %>")
# run template
ERB.new(madlib).run
```

The main principle here is to convert ((...)) to <%= ... %>, so we can use ERB. Of course, <%= a noun %> isn't going to be valid Ruby code, so a helper method is needed. That's where q_to_a() comes in. It takes the Mad Libs replacements as an argument and returns the user's answer. To use that, we actually need to convert ((...)) to <%= q_to_a('...') %>. From there, ERB does the rest of the work for us.

Custom Templating

Now for simple Mad Libs, you don't really need something as robust as ERB. It's easy to roll your own solution, and most people did just that. Let's examine a custom parsing program.

There are really only three kinds of story elements in our Mad Libs exercise. There's ordinary prose, questions to ask the user, and reused replacement values.

The last of those is the easiest to identify, so let's start there. If a value between the ((...)) placeholders has already been set by a question, it is a replacement. That's easy enough to translate to code:

```
code/madlibs/parsed_madlib.rb
# A placeholder in the story for a reused value.
class Replacement
  # Only if we have a replacement for a given token is this class a match.
  def self.parse?( token, replacements )
    if token[0..1] == "((" and replacements.include? token[2..-1]
      new(token[2..-1], replacements)
    else
      false
    end
  end

  def initialize( name, replacements )
    @name         = name
    @replacements = replacements
  end

  def to_s
    @replacements[@name]
  end
end
```

Using parse?(), you can turn a replacement value from the story into a code element that can later be used to build the final story. The return value of parse?() is either **false**, if the token was not a replacement value, or the constructed Replacement object.

Inside parse?(), a token is selected if it begins with a ((and the name is in the Hash of replacements. When that is the case, the name and Hash are stored so the lookup can be made when the time comes. That lookup is the to_s() method.

On to Question objects:

```
code/madlibs/parsed_madlib.rb
# A question for the user, to be replaced with their answer.
class Question
  # If we see a ((, it's a prompt.  Save their answer if a name is given.
  def self.parse?( prompt, replacements )
    if prompt.sub!(/^\(\(/, "")
      prompt, name = prompt.split(":").reverse
```

```
      replacements[name] = nil unless name.nil?

      new(prompt, name, replacements)
    else
      false
    end
  end

  def initialize( prompt, name, replacements )
    @prompt       = prompt
    @name         = name
    @replacements = replacements
  end

  def to_s
    print "Enter #{@prompt}:   "
    answer = $stdin.gets.to_s.strip

    @replacements[@name] = answer unless @name.nil?

    answer
  end
end
```

A Question is identified as any token left in the story that starts with ((
and wasn't a Replacement. The prompt and name, if there was one, are
stored alone with the replacements for later use. A **nil** value is added
under a requested name in the Hash, so future Replacement objects will
match.

When the to_s() method is called, Question will query the user and return
the answer. It will also set the value in the @replacements, if the question
was named.

Stories have only one more element: the prose. Ruby already has an
object for that, a String. Let's just adapt String's interface so we can use
it:

`code/madlibs/parsed_madlib.rb`
```
# Ordinary prose.
class String
  # Anything is acceptable.
  def self.parse?( token, replacements )
    new(token)
  end
end
```

No surprises there. All elements left in the story are prose, so parse?()
accepts anything, returning a simple string.

Here's the application code that completes the solution:

```
code/madlibs/parsed_madlib.rb
# argument parsing
unless ARGV.size == 1 and test(?e, ARGV[0])
  puts "Usage:  #{File.basename($PROGRAM_NAME)} MADLIB_FILE"
  exit
end
madlib = <<MADLIB

#{File.basename(ARGV.first, ".madlib").tr("_", " ")}

#{File.read(ARGV.first)}
MADLIB

# tokenize input
tokens = madlib.split(/(\(\(\([^)]+)\)\))/).map do |token|
  token[0..1] == "((" ? token.gsub(/\s+/, " ") : token
end

# identify each part of the story
answers = Hash.new
story   = tokens.map do |token|
  [Replacement, Question, String].inject(false) do |element, kind|
    element = kind.parse?(token, answers) and break element
  end
end

# share the results
puts story.join
```

After some familiar argument-parsing code, we find a three-stage process for going from input to finished story. First, the input file is broken down into tokens. Tokenization is really just a single call to split(). It's important to note that anything captured by parentheses in the Regexp used by split() is part of the returned set. This is used to return ((...)) tokens, even though they are the delimiter for split(). However, the capturing parentheses are placed to drop the trailing)). The leading ((is kept for later token identification. Finally, whitespace is normalized inside ((...)) tokens, in case they run over multiple lines.

In the second stage, each token is converted into a Replacement, Question, or String object by the rules we defined earlier. Don't let that funny-looking inject() call throw you. I could have just used a body of element or kind.parse?(token, answers), but that keeps checking all the classes even after it has found a match. The **break** was added to short-circuit the process as soon as we find a parser that accepts the token.

The final stage of processing actually creates and displays a story. In

order to understand that single line of code, you need to know that join()
will ensure all the elements are String objects, by calling to_s() on them,
before adding them together.

It's probably worth noting that while this parsing process is some-
what more involved than the other solutions we have and will examine,
only the final step needs to be repeated if we wanted to run the same
story again, say for a different user. The parsed format is completely
reusable.

Mini Libs

Let's examine one more super small solution by Dominik Bathon. Obviously, this code is a round of golf[23] and not what most of us would
consider pretty, but it still contains some interesting ideas:

```
code/madlibs/golfed_madlib.rb
keys=Hash.new { |h, k|
    puts "Give me #{k.sub(/\A([^:]+):/, "")}:"
    h[$1]=$stdin.gets.chomp
}
puts "", $*[0].split(".")[0].gsub("_", " "),
    IO.read($*[0]).gsub(/\(\(([^)]+)\)\)/) { keys[$1] }
```

In order to understand this code, start at the final puts() call. You don't
see it used too often, but Ruby's puts() will accept a list of lines to print.
This code is using that. The first of the three lines is just an empty
String that yields a blank line before we print the story.

The second line puts() is asked to print is the Mad Lib's name itself,
which is pulled from the file name. The key to understanding this snippet is to know that the Perlish variable $* is a synonym for ARGV. Given
that, you can see the first command-line argument is read, stripped of
an extension with split(), and cleaned up ("_" to " " translation). The end
result is a human readable title.

The last line is actually the entire Mad Libs story. Again, you see it
accessed through the first member of $*. The gsub() call handles the
question asking and replacement in one clever step using a simple Hash.

Let's take a closer look at that Hash. Jump back to the beginning of the
program now. The Hash uses a default value block to conjure key-value

---

[23] *Golf* is a sport programmers sometimes engage in to code a solution in a minimal
amount of keystrokes. They will often use surprising code constructs, as long as it shaves
off a few characters. Because of this, the resulting program can be difficult to read.

pairs as they are needed. It prints a question, sub()ing a key name out if needed. You can see that the answer is read from the user and shoved right into the Hash under the $1 key. Exactly what's in that $1 variable is the trick. Notice that the original gsub() from the lower puts() call sets $1 to the entire Mad Libs question. However, the Hash block sometimes performs another substitution, which overwrites $1. If the substitution was named, $1 would be set to that name. Otherwise, the sub() call will fail, and $1 will be unaltered. Then, because we're talking about a Hash here, future access to the same key will just return the set value, bypassing the tricky block.

Again, the above previous has a few bad habits, but it also uses some rare and interesting Ruby idioms to do a lot of work in very little code.

Additional Exercises

1. Extend the Mad Libs syntax to support case changes.

2. Enhance your solution to support the new syntax.

Answer 2

From page 9

LCD Numbers

Clearly this problem isn't too difficult. Hao (David) Tran sent in a golfed solution (not shown) in less than 300 bytes. Easy or not, this classic challenge does address topics such as scaling and joining multiline data that are applicable to many areas of computer programming.

Using Templates

I've seen three main strategies used for solving the problem. Some use a template approach, where you have some kind of text representation of your number at a scale of one. Two might look like this, for example:

```
[ " - ",
  "   |",
  " - ",
  "|   ",
  " - " ]
```

Scaling that to any size is a twofold process. First, you need to stretch it horizontally. The easy way to do that is to grab the second character of each string (a "-" or a " ") and repeat it -s times:

```
digit.each { |row| row[1, 1] *= scale }
```

After that, the digit needs to be scaled vertically. That's pretty easy to do while printing it out, if you want. Just print any line containing a | -s times:

```
digit.each do |row|
  if row.include? "|"
    scale.times { puts row }
  else
    puts row
  end
end
```

Here's a complete solution, drawing those ideas together:

```
code/lcd_numbers/template.rb
# templates
DIGITS = <<END_DIGITS.split("\n").map { |row| row.split(" # ") }.transpose
 -  #    #  -  #  -  #    #  -  #  -  #  -  #  -  #  -
 | | #   | #   | #   | # | | # |   # |   #   | # | | # | |
    #    #  -  #  -  #  -  #  -  #    #  -  #  -
 | | #   | # |  #   | # | | #   | # | | #   | # | | #   |
 -  #    #  -  #  -  #    #  -  #  -  #    #  -  #  -
END_DIGITS


# number scaling (horizontally and vertically)
def scale( num, size )
  bigger = [ ]
  num.each do |line|
    row = line.dup
    row[1, 1] *= size
    if row.include? "/"
      size.times { bigger << row }
    else
      bigger << row
    end
  end
  bigger
end


# option parsing
s = 2
if ARGV.size >= 2 and ARGV[0] == '-s' and ARGV[1] =~ /^[1-9]\d*$/
  ARGV.shift
  s = ARGV.shift.to_i
end


# digit parsing/usage
unless ARGV.size == 1 and ARGV[0] =~ /^\d+$/
  puts "Usage:  #$0 [-s SIZE] DIGITS"
  exit
end
n = ARGV.shift


# scaling
num = [ ]
n.each_byte do |c|
  num << [" "] * (s * 2 + 3) if num.size > 0
  num << scale(DIGITS[c.chr.to_i], s)
end


# output
num = ([""] * (s * 2 + 3)).zip(*num)
num.each { |l| puts l.join }
```

On and Off Bits

A second strategy used is to treat each digit as a series of segments that can be on or off. The numbers easily break down into seven positions:

```
  6
5   4
  3
2   1
  0
```

Using that map, we can convert the representation of 2 to binary:

```
0b1011101
```

Expansion of these representations is handled much as it was in the previous approach. Here's a complete solution using bits by Florian Groß:

```
code/lcd_numbers/bits.rb
module LCD
  extend self

  # Digits are represented by simple bit masks. Each bit identifies
  # whether a line should be displayed. The following ASCII
  # graphic shows the mapping from bit position to the belonging line.
  #
  #   =6
  # 5   4
  #   =3
  # 2   1
  #   =0
  Digits = [0b1110111, 0b0100100, 0b1011101, 0b1101101, 0b0101110,
            0b1101011, 0b1111011, 0b0100101, 0b1111111, 0b1101111,
            0b0001000, 0b1111000] # Minus, Dot
  Top, TopLeft, TopRight, Middle, BottomLeft, BottomRight, Bottom = *0 .. 6
  SpecialDigits = { "-" => 10, "." => 11 }


  private

  def line(digit, bit, char = "/")
    (digit & 1 << bit).zero? ? " " : char
  end

  def horizontal(digit, size, bit)
    [" " + line(digit, bit, "-") * size + " "]
  end

  def vertical(digit, size, left_bit, right_bit)
    [line(digit, left_bit) + " " * size + line(digit, right_bit)] * size
  end
```

```ruby
  def digit(digit, size)
    digit = Digits[digit.to_i]
    horizontal(digit, size, Top) +
    vertical(digit, size, TopLeft, TopRight) +
    horizontal(digit, size, Middle) +
    vertical(digit, size, BottomLeft, BottomRight) +
    horizontal(digit, size, Bottom)
  end

  public

  def render(number, size = 1)
    number = number.to_s
    raise(ArgumentError, "size has to be > 0") unless size > 0
    raise(ArgumentError, "Invalid number") unless number[/\A[\d.-]+\Z/]

    number.scan(/./).map do |digit|
      digit(SpecialDigits[digit] || digit, size)
    end.transpose.map do |line|
      line.join(" ")
    end.join("\n")
  end
end

if __FILE__ == $0
  require 'optparse'
  options = { :size => 2 }
  number = ARGV.pop

  ARGV.options do |opts|
    script_name = File.basename($0)
    opts.banner = "Usage: ruby #{script_name} [options] number"

    opts.separator ""

    opts.on("-s", "-size size", Numeric,
      "Specify the size of line segments.",
      "Default: 2"
    ) { |options[:size]| }

    opts.separator ""

    opts.on("-h", "-help", "Show this help message.") { puts opts; exit }

    opts.parse!
  end

  puts LCD.render(number, options[:size])
end
```

With either method, you will need to join the scaled digits together for output. This is basically a two-dimensional join() problem. Building a routine like that is simple using either Array.zip() or Array.transpose().

Using a State Machine

Finally, a unique third strategy involves a state machine. Let's look at the primary class of Dale Martenson's solution:

Spring Cleaning

I altered the LCD class to use constants instead of class variables. This seemed closer to their intended purpose.

`code/lcd_numbers/states.rb`

```ruby
class LCD

  # This hash defines the segment display for the given digit. Each
  # entry in the array is associated with the following states:
  #
  #   HORIZONTAL
  #   VERTICAL
  #   HORIZONTAL
  #   VERTICAL
  #   HORIZONTAL
  #   DONE
  #
  # The HORIZONTAL state produces a single horizontal line. There
  # are two types:
  #
  #   0 - skip, no line necessary, just space fill
  #   1 - line required of given size
  #
  # The VERTICAL state produces either a single right side line,
  # a single left side line or both lines.
  #
  #   0 - skip, no line necessary, just space fill
  #   1 - single right side line
  #   2 - single left side line
  #   3 - both lines
  #
  # The DONE state terminates the state machine. This is not needed
  # as part of the data array.
  LCD_DISPLAY_DATA = {
    "0" => [ 1, 3, 0, 3, 1 ],
    "1" => [ 0, 1, 0, 1, 0 ],
    "2" => [ 1, 1, 1, 2, 1 ],
    "3" => [ 1, 1, 1, 1, 1 ],
    "4" => [ 0, 3, 1, 1, 0 ],
    "5" => [ 1, 2, 1, 1, 1 ],
    "6" => [ 1, 2, 1, 3, 1 ],
    "7" => [ 1, 1, 0, 1, 0 ],
    "8" => [ 1, 3, 1, 3, 1 ],
    "9" => [ 1, 3, 1, 1, 1 ]
  }
```

```ruby
LCD_STATES = [
  "HORIZONTAL",
  "VERTICAL",
  "HORIZONTAL",
  "VERTICAL",
  "HORIZONTAL",
  "DONE"
]

attr_accessor :size, :spacing

def initialize( size=1, spacing=1 )
  @size = size
  @spacing = spacing
end

def display( digits )
  states = LCD_STATES.reverse
  0.upto(LCD_STATES.length) do |i|
    case states.pop
    when "HORIZONTAL"
      line = ""
      digits.each_byte do |b|
        line += horizontal_segment( LCD_DISPLAY_DATA[b.chr][i] )
      end
      print line + "\n"
    when "VERTICAL"
      1.upto(@size) do |j|
        line = ""
        digits.each_byte do |b|
          line += vertical_segment( LCD_DISPLAY_DATA[b.chr][i] )
        end
        print line + "\n"
      end
    when "DONE"
      break
    end
  end
end

def horizontal_segment( type )
  case type
  when 1
    return " " + ("-" * @size) + " " + (" " * @spacing)
  else
    return " " + (" " * @size) + " " + (" " * @spacing)
  end
end
```

```ruby
  def vertical_segment( type )
    case type
    when 1
      return " " + ( " " * @size) + "/" + ( " " * @spacing)
    when 2
      return "/" + ( " " * @size) + " " + ( " " * @spacing)
    when 3
      return "/" + ( " " * @size) + "/" + ( " " * @spacing)
    else
      return " " + ( " " * @size) + " " + ( " " * @spacing)
    end
  end
end
```

The comment at the beginning of the LCD class gives you a nice clue to what is going on here. The class represents a state machine. For the needed size (set in initialize()), the class walks a series of states (defined in LCD_STATES). At each state, horizontal and vertical segments are built as needed (with horizontal_segment() and vertical_segment()).

The process I've just described is run through display(), the primary interface method. You pass it a string of digits, and it walks each state and generates segments as needed.

One nice aspect of this approach is that it's easy to handle output one line at a time, as shown in display(). The top line of all digits, generated by the first "HORIZONTAL" state, is printed as soon as it's built, as is each state that follows. This resource-friendly system could scale well to much larger inputs.

The rest of Dale's code is option parsing and the call to display():

`code/lcd_numbers/states.rb`
```ruby
require 'getoptlong'

opts = GetoptLong.new(
  [ "-size", "-s", GetoptLong::REQUIRED_ARGUMENT ],
  [ "-spacing", "-sp", "-p", GetoptLong::REQUIRED_ARGUMENT ]
)

lcd = LCD.new

opts.each do |opt, arg|
  case opt
  when "-size"    then lcd.size = arg.to_i
  when "-spacing" then lcd.spacing = arg.to_i
  end
end

lcd.display( ARGV.shift )
```

Additional Exercises

1. Modify your solution to print each line as it is built instead of building up the whole number, if it doesn't already.

2. Extend Florian Groß's solution to add the hexadecimal digits A through F.

Answer 3
From page 11

GEDCOM Parser

Let's jump right into a solution submitted by Hans Fugal:

`code/gedcom_parser/simple.rb`

```ruby
#! /usr/bin/ruby
require 'rexml/document'

doc = REXML::Document.new "<gedcom/>"
stack = [doc.root]

ARGF.each_line do |line|
  next if line =~ /^\s*$/

  # parse line
  line =~ /^\s*([0-9]+)\s+(@\S+@|\S+)(\s(.*))?$/ or raise "Invalid GEDCOM"
  level = $1.to_i
  tag = $2
  data = $4

  # pop off the stack until we get the parent
  while (level+1) < stack.size
    stack.pop
  end
  parent = stack.last

  # create XML tag
  if tag =~ /@.+@/
    el = parent.add_element data
    el.attributes['id'] = tag
  else
    el = parent.add_element tag
    el.text = data
  end

  stack.push el
end
doc.write($stdout,0)
puts
```

This code uses the standard REXML library.[24] This is a tool for parsing (or in this case, generating) XML documents. The usage here is very basic. First a document is created, and then elements are added to it as they are built. At the end, the completed document is written to $stdout.

The previous starts by creating a REXML document and a stack for managing parent/child relationships. The stack is just an Array, which is quite versatile in Ruby. With setup out of the way, the code reads from $stdin or files specified as command-line arguments, line by line. That's exactly what the ARGF object is for.

Each line is processed in three stages. The first step is to parse the line. Hans uses a Regexp to break down the line and then assigns the capture variables to level, tag, and data.

The second step is to rewind the stack until we find the parent element for this line. That makes sure the following code will add the current element to the correct place in the XML document.

The third and final step does that addition. Here the line data is checked for the two possible formats defined in the quiz. REXML is used to create an element for the proper format[25] and add that element to the parent element. The stack is then updated with the new element.

When it has all been read, the complete XML is dumped to $stdout.

Optimizing the Read and Write Cycles

One problem with using REXML is that the entire document must be constructed before it can be output. With large GEDCOM files and REXML needing to store the information it does, this can exhaust available memory for some systems. If you want to get around that, you'll need to build up your own XML strings. The advantage of this is that you can output nodes as soon as you have seen all their children (when the LEVEL drops). This is pretty efficient. Let's take a look at a solution from Jamis Buck that used that technique:

```
code/gedcom_parser/efficient.rb
#!/usr/bin/env ruby
```

---

[24]You can read the online documentation for REXML at http://www.germane-software.com/software/rexml/docs/tutorial.html.

[25]If you aren't going to use a great library like REXML to generate XML output, remember to handle your own escaping! This was a common mistake in submitted solutions. You can even use REXML for escaping only: REXML::Text.normalize("Some & text < foo > \" bar").

GEDCOM Specifics

Obviously, Hans's solution doesn't do any special handling of the GEDCOM format. It's a simple parse and print solution. Some solutions may want to interpret more from the GEDCOM file as opposed to simple translation. For example, a solution could build a single entity out of GEDCOM's CONC and CONT fields. Those fields represent a continuation of long data elements. Of course, techniques like this require some knowledge of the GEDCOM format beyond what is given in the quiz.

```ruby
class GED2XML

  IS_ID = /^@.*@$/

  class Node < Struct.new( :level, :tag, :data, :refid )
    def initialize( line=nil )
      level, tag, data = line.chomp.split( /\s+/, 3 )
      level = level.to_i
      tag, refid, data = data, tag, nil if tag =~ IS_ID
      super level, tag.downcase, data, refid
    end
  end

  def indent( level )
    print "   " * ( level + 1 )
  end

  def safe( text )
    text.
      gsub( /&/,  "&amp;" ).
      gsub( /</,  "&lt;" ).
      gsub( />/,  "&gt;" ).
      gsub( /"/,  "&quot;" )
  end

  def process( io )
    node_stack = []

    puts "<gedcom>"
    wrote_newline = true

    io.each_line do |line|
      next if line =~ /^\s*$/o
      node = Node.new( line )
```

```
    while !node_stack.empty? && node_stack.last.level >= node.level
      prev = node_stack.pop
      indent prev.level if wrote_newline
      print "</#{prev.tag}>\n"
      wrote_newline = true
    end

    indent node.level if wrote_newline
    print "<#{node.tag}"
    print " id=\"#{node.refid}\"" if node.refid

    if node.data
      if node.data =~ IS_ID
        print " ref=\"#{node.data}\">"
      else
        print ">#{safe(node.data)}"
      end
      wrote_newline = false
    else
      puts ">"
      wrote_newline = true
    end

    node_stack << node
  end

  until node_stack.empty?
    prev = node_stack.pop
    indent prev.level if wrote_newline
    print "</#{prev.tag}>\n"
    wrote_newline = true
  end

  puts "</gedcom>"
  end

end

GED2XML.new.process ARGF
```

The first thing that jumps out of this code is the inner class Node. Jamis wants to use a Struct here, but he wants it to be capable of finding the data it needs in a given line. To set that up, Node inherits directly from a constructor call.Struct.new returns the Class object it created, which is immediately used as a parent class for the inheritance of Node. Think of this as anonymous inheritance. In Node's initialize() method, the data is broken down as needed and then handed off to the standard constructor for a Struct.

Next, GED2XML defines a couple of helper methods. The indent() method is just a tool for keeping the XML output pretty by printing an indent for the current level of the hierarchy. The safe() method is needed because we won't be able to count on REXML to handle escaping this time around. It returns a copy of the passed-in String that is properly escaped XML (as long as you store the attributes in double quotes).

We then come to the process() method, where most of the work is done. This is similar to the solution we examined from Hans earlier. There are only a few differences:

- Output is printed directly, instead of using REXML to build elements.

- When popping elements off the stack, we need to print a closing tag for that element.

- That means we have to clear the stack one final time after the parsing is done to ensure that all elements are closed.

That's all there is to that solution. As you can see, the last line simply hands ARGF to process() to trigger the transform.

Again, the second solution is more efficient and can handle bigger data on smaller hardware. However, the first one is a little easier to build and may be all you need in many cases. "Use the simplest thing that could possibly work," as the eXtreme Programming crowd is fond of saying.

Additional Exercises

1. Compare the run-time and memory usage of the two solutions discussed previously and your own. Note the differences.

2. Reverse the process of this quiz. Read in the XML you generated, and output a GEDCOM file, formatted like the examples in the quiz.

Answer <big>**4**</big>
From page 13

Animal Quiz

Everybody solved this one using pretty much the same technique. Jim Weirich explains the strategy:

> *There is an easy solution that represents the database as a binary tree with questions as interior nodes and possible animals as leaf nodes. Each interior question node has two children corresponding to a "yes" or "no" answer. The children are either further questions (which will be asked) or an animal (which will be guessed).*

Couldn't have said it better myself. Let's see Jim's own implementation of said tree:

> **Spring Cleaning**
> *I removed the letter y from the vowels in Animal.an(), because all but the most obscure words starting with y should still use a as an article (for example, a yew).*

code/animal_quiz/animals.rb
```ruby
#!/usr/bin/env ruby
require 'yaml'
require 'ui'

def ui
  $ui ||= ConsoleUi.new
end

class Question
  def initialize(question, yes, no)
    @question = question
    @yes = yes
    @no = no
    @question << "?" unless @question =~ /\?$/
    @question.sub!(/^([a-z])/) { $1.upcase }
  end

  def walk
    if ui.ask_if @question
      @yes = @yes.walk
    else
      @no = @no.walk
    end
```

```ruby
        self
      end
    end

    class Animal
      attr_reader :name
      def initialize(name)
        @name = name
      end

      def walk
        if ui.ask_if "Is it #{an name}?"
          ui.say "Yea!  I win!\n\n"
          self
        else
          ui.say "Rats, I lose"
          ui.say "Help me play better next time."
          new_animal = ui.ask "What animal were you thinking of?"
          question = ui.ask "Give me a question " +
                            "to distinguish a #{an name} from #{an new_animal}."
          response = ui.ask_if "For #{an new_animal}, " +
                               "the answer to your question would be?"
          ui.say "Thank you\n\n"
          if response
            Question.new(question, Animal.new(new_animal), self)
          else
            Question.new(question, self, Animal.new(new_animal))
          end
        end
      end

      def an(animal)
        ((animal =~ /^[aeiou]/) ? "an " : "a ") + animal
      end
    end

    if File.exist? "animals.yaml"
      current = open("animals.yaml") { |f| YAML.load(f.read) }
    else
      current = Animal.new("mouse")
    end

    loop do
      current = current.walk
      break unless ui.ask_if "Play again?"
      ui.say "\n\n"
    end

    open("animals.yaml", "w") do |f| f.puts current.to_yaml end
```

This is a very straightforward solution. At the top, it brings in YAML for storage (many people did this) and a ui library to handle the interface. It also defines a helper method for the ui library, making it trivial to change the entire interface just by setting a global variable.

Skip over the class definitions now, and have a look at the "main" section. The first third loads an existing animal tree, if one is available. Otherwise, it creates a new tree.

The middle third walks the tree, saving the result in case a new node is added. It then asks whether the user would like to play again, using the ui() helper method.

The last third uses YAML to save out the tree at the end of this run.

To make sense of all this talk about a "tree," you need to go back up and examine the two classes. As described in the strategy quote, Question objects hold the question itself, as well as links to the answer nodes for "yes" and "no". The real method of interest here is Question.walk() (not to be confused with Animal.walk(), which we will examine shortly). walk() asks its question through ui() and then recurses into @yes.walk() or @no.walk(), depending on the answer provided. The trick to note here is that the result of the call is saved back to the node. That allows nodes to update themselves when the game learns a new animal.

That just leaves Animal, which is even easier to grasp. Again, the method of interest is Animal.walk(). walk() guesses the animal over ui() and declares victory if it's right. When it's wrong, it asks the clarifying questions to learn and returns itself and the new animal wrapped in a new Question object. This return ensures that the tree is updated, thanks to the saving behavior of Question.walk().

That leaves only the mystical ui library. Here's a look at it:

`code/animal_quiz/ui.rb`

```ruby
#!/usr/bin/env ruby

class ConsoleUi
  def ask(prompt)
    print prompt + " "
    answer = gets
    answer ? answer.chomp : nil
  end

  def ask_if(prompt)
    answer = ask(prompt)
    answer =~ /^\s*[Yy]/
  end

  def say(*msg)
```

```
      puts msg
    end
  end
```

This is just a console interface, of course. ask() handles input, say() handles output, and ask_if() is a helper method that returns true if it looks like the user answered with a "yes" or false otherwise (handy for if conditions, thus the name). These methods could be replaced with CGI equivalents, GUI routines, or whatever. Nice abstraction here.

Arrays Instead of Custom Objects

That's a nice object-oriented abstraction for the tree, but you could also use simple data structures to solve the quiz. Let's look at a version by Markus König that uses nested Arrays:

code/animal_quiz/array.rb
```ruby
#! /usr/bin/env ruby

def ask(prompt)
  loop do
    print prompt, ' '
    $stdout.flush
    s = gets
    exit if s == nil
    s.chomp!
    if s == 'y' or s == 'yes'
      return true
    elsif s == 'n' or s == 'no'
      return false
    else
      $stderr.puts "Please answer yes or no."
    end
  end
end

def my_readline
  s = gets
  exit if s == nil
  s.chomp!
  return s
end

class AnimalQuiz
  DEFAULT_ANSWERS = ['an elephant']

  def initialize(filename)
    if not filename
      @answers = DEFAULT_ANSWERS
    else
```

```ruby
    begin
      File.open(filename) do |f|
        @answers = eval(f.read)
      end
    rescue Errno::ENOENT
      @answers = DEFAULT_ANSWERS
    end
  end


  @current = nil
end

def save(filename)
  File.open(filename, 'w') do |f|
    f.puts @answers.inspect
  end
end

def run_once
  unless @current
    @current = @answers
    puts 'Think of an animal...'
  end

  if @current.length == 1
    if ask("Is it #{@current[0]}?")
      puts 'I win!  Pretty smart, aren\'t I?'
    else
      print 'You win!  Help me learn from my '
      puts 'mistake before you go...'
      puts 'What animal were you thinking of?'
      correct = my_readline
      incorrect = @current[0]
      print 'Give me a question to distinguish '
      puts "#{correct} from #{incorrect}."
      question = my_readline
      if ask("For #{correct}, what is the" \
          + ' answer to your question?')
        @current.push [correct]
        @current.push [incorrect]
      else
        @current.push [incorrect]
        @current.push [correct]
      end
      @current[0] = question
    end
    if ask('Play again?')
      @current = nil
      puts
    else
      exit
```

```ruby
      end
    elsif @current.length == 3
      if ask(@current[0])
        @current = @current[1]
      else
        @current = @current[2]
      end
    end
  end

  def run
    loop {run_once}
  end
end

filename = ENV['HOME'] + '/.animal-quiz'

quiz = AnimalQuiz.new(filename)
begin
  quiz.run
ensure
  quiz.save filename
end
```

This code starts with a couple of utility methods. The first, ask(), gets a valid "yes" or "no" answer from the user through the terminal. Notice how it loops until given a valid answer and then uses **return** to break out of the loop.

The other method, my_readline(), is an auto-chomp()ing version of gets(). This makes asking the user questions easier later.

The AnimalQuiz class contains the majority of the solution. It starts by setting a default answer tree, which is just a simple Array. You can see that initialize() tries to load a previously saved tree but uses the default if this cannot be done (possibly because no file exists in the first run).

Take a good look at that file load in initialize() before we move on. Aside from the pretty exception handling, what is it really loading? Ruby code. Smooth. If you jump down to save(), you'll see how the Array is saved out to the file as actual code. Then initialize() can just eval() it to re-create it.[26]

---

[26]It's always good to remember that eval(), while helpful, can be dangerous, and using it should always be considered carefully. There's probably not a lot of risk in this instance, but it's important to note that should malicious Ruby code be added the program's saved file, it will be blindly executed the next time the program is launched.

The run_once() method is the heart of this solution. On the first call, it sets @current to the answer tree Array, and then it forks depending on whether the tree has one or three members. A one-member Array is an animal, so it's guessed, and the user is asked whether the program was correct. If it was, the current game ends with a final printed message. If not, the user is asked to give the correct animal. Note how these answers are saved. The "yes" and "no" branch answers are added to @current, and the animal is replaced with the new question. This converts the current Array in the tree from one to three members. Now the added branches are wrapped in Arrays when added, to keep the tree growing.

When the current Array of the tree has three members, we know it's a question. The program asks and branches to the next Array of the tree based on the answer.

The run() method turns run_once() into a cycle of games with repeated execution. The rest of the code just loads the previous file and kicks off the run() method. Look at the nice use of **ensure** here to perform the final save when quitting. This is essential, since exit() can be called any time the user is asked for input.

Leaving the Trees

Now, I did say the tree method was easy, but it's not without its faults. Once more, I give you the voice of Jim:

> The tree solution has some drawbacks. It is very sensitive to the order in which animals are added to the tree and the type of questions used. The tree solution works best when the early questions divide the set of possible animals into more or less equal groups. This keeps the tree nicely balanced, and the series of questions leading up to any guess are all equally short. Unfortunately, in real life the tree tends to become very unbalanced with individual questions targeting a rather specific animal in the "yes" branch and the "no" branch becoming a long list of more specific questions.

> Another small problem with the tree solution is that some questions are ambiguous, or the user doesn't have the knowledge to answer the question properly. For example, a question might be "Does it live in the water?" Some people might select a beaver as their animal and think "Oh yes, it loves to swim." Others might say "No, it lives on land, it just enjoys swimming." In actual practice, these ambiguities average out and you would get the beaver answer on both "yes" and "no" nodes of a question, each branch using different questions

to narrow down the choice. Although not a fatal flaw, it does put redundant answers in the tree and essentially waste a question that could be put to better use.

I actually did a fair amount of thinking about other approaches to this problem. Unfortunately, every time I broke from the tree structure, it became a lot trickier to add new animals. I basically had to badger the user for answers to half of all the questions known about their animal, and in doing so it seemed I ran into even more irrelevancy issues. Because of that, I eventually abandoned the approach. If anybody has or creates another strategy for this, be sure to share![27]

Additional Exercises

1. Get as many different people as you can to play with your solution. Take it to your son's school show-and-tell, wrap it in a web interface[28] and get the whole world using it, or just drag all the visitors to your home back to the keyboard for a few quick guesses. Examine the tree after so many people have altered it.

2. Add a history feature to the program so that it can tell you how many times it has correctly guessed an animal.

3. Modify your program so you can ask it to tell you about an animal it knows of and have it respond with as many details as possible. For example:

```
⇐   describe mouse
⇒   A mouse is small.
    A mouse does not fly.
    A mouse has fur.
```

You may need to rethink animal entry details to support this.

---

[27]I'm told that http://20q.net/ uses a nonhierarchical approach for its game.
[28]See http://www.animalgame.com/play/ for an example.

Answer 5
From page 15

Scrabble Stems

We can solve the Scrabble stem problem without much effort using the typical algorithm trade-off. We can sacrifice memory (in some cases it's speed, or even both) for an easy-to-code solution. There are a lot of stems, but we can generate them all and store them with around 50 MB of RAM, which is not too rare these days.

Let's see how that turns out:

`code/scrabble_stems/in_memory.rb`

```ruby
#!/usr/local/bin/ruby -w

# argument parsing
DICTIONARY = if ARGV.first == "-w"
  ARGV.shift
  ARGV.shift
else
  "/usr/share/dict/words"
end
if ARGV.first =~ /\A\d+\Z/
  LIMIT = ARGV.first.to_i
else
  puts "Usage:  #{File.basename($PROGRAM_NAME)} [-d DICTIONARY_FILE] LIMIT"
  exit
end

# storage for all the stems we find and the letters they combine with
stems = Hash.new

# read the dictionary
File.foreach(DICTIONARY) do |word|
  # clean up the words
  word.downcase!
  word.delete!("^a-z")

  # skip anything but a seven letter word
  next unless word.length == 7
```

```ruby
# translate word to an alphabetized arrangement of letters
signature = word.split(//).sort
# remove each letter from the word to create stems
signature.uniq.each do |letter|
  stem = signature.join.sub(letter, "")
  (stems[stem] ||= Hash.new)[letter] = true
end
end

# drop anything below the limit and reorder
result = stems.reject { |stem, combines| combines.size < LIMIT }.
          sort_by { |stem, combines| -combines.size }

# display the results
result.each do |stem, combines|
  puts "#{stem} (#{combines.size}) #{combines.keys.sort.join}"
end
```

The code starts by setting up DICTIONARY and LIMIT constants for the program arguments. It also creates a Hash to hold the stems it will find.

After that, we read the dictionary, line by line. This is where most of the work is done. The code inside foreach() normalizes case, tosses out any punctuation and whitespace, and checks to make sure we keep only seven-letter words. The next step is to split() the words into letters and sort() them, creating a signature that will match other words using the same letters (anagrams). Then we remove the unique letters from the word one at a time to find all the stems, adding each of those to stems.

At this point we've found all the stems in the dictionary for all seven-letter words. The next chunk of code removes results below the limit we wanted and sorts the results for display.

The final chunk of the program writes out the results, line by line.

Of course, we can't always afford to sacrifice the RAM. And this problem could be solved without as much memory. The trick for that is to generate and verify stems one at a time. This might be needed if the search space was larger.

Eating Less RAM

Let's examine a less obvious solution that's a little friendlier on memory and a touch faster. Here's some code by Dennis Ranke:

Spring Cleaning

I replaced a couple of magic number 97s with ?as, because I suspect it makes their purpose more obvious to readers.

`code/scrabble_stems/bit_work.rb`
```ruby
hash = Hash.new {|h, k| h[k] = 0}
File.foreach(ARGV[0] || 'WORD.LST') do |line|
```

```
      line.strip!
      if line.size == 7
        letters = line.downcase.scan(/./).sort.join
        7.times do |i|
          hash[letters[0, i] + letters[(i+1)..-1]] |= 1 << (letters[i] - ?a)
        end
      end
    end

cutoff = (ARGV[1] || '15').to_i
count = {}
hash.each do |k, v|
  v = (v & 0x5555555) + ((v>>1) & 0x5555555)
  v = (v & 0x3333333) + ((v>>2) & 0x3333333)
  v = (v & 0xf0f0f0f) + ((v>>4) & 0xf0f0f0f)
  v = (v & 0x0ff00ff) + ((v>>8) & 0x0ff00ff)
  v = (v & 0x000ffff) + ((v>>16) & 0x000ffff)
  count[k] = v if v >= cutoff
end

count.keys.sort_by {|k| count[k]}.each do |letters|
  printf "%s: (%d) ", letters, count[letters]
  combi = hash[letters]
  26.times do |i|
    print((i+?a).chr) if combi[i] == 1
  end
  puts
end
```

It's pretty clear at first glance that first foreach() is loading hash, but what are the keys and values? The first couple of lines in that iterator throw away whitespace and ensure that we deal only with seven-letter words. You can then see that this code breaks words down into letters, just as the other version did, but uses scan() for the job instead of split(). Then we come to the hash loading.

Since hash loading happens in a 7.times do ... end block, we can probably assume it's working letter by letter. In fact, i seems to be the index of each letter. That should help us break down the key for the hash. The first half of the key is a substring indexed with index and length. That should fetch all the letters before the current letter. (Note that the first iteration will fetch letters[0, 0] which will give "".) The second half of the key is everything after the current letter, of course. So the key is our six-letter stem. Now we need the value.

First we need to notice that values aren't simply assigned. They use |= for a bitwise OR and then assignment. (The first line of the script has hash elements default to 0 to support this.) The old value is ORed with a 1, shifted by the letter's ASCII value minus the ASCII value of a. That creates a bitmap of all the letters in the alphabet. Using a single integer, bits are flipped on for each letter that matches up with this stem.

That middle section of the code looks scarier than it is. It's loading the count Hash with some transformation of hash. That transformation is hidden in a lot of arcane constants, bitwise ANDs, and bit shifting by magic number offsets. However, the end result is that it turns the bitmap values into a count of matches. Put another way, you could replace all five v = ... lines with v = sprintf("%b", v).count("1") and get identical answers. Stems are moved over to the count Hash only if their count is above the cutoff.

The final third of the script prints the results. First we get a stem and a count, and then the bit map is walked to produce a list of all characters this stem combines with.

That gives us a little more information than the previous script. It also works faster since computers do bit math so fast and uses a little less memory, thanks to the bitmap. Of course, it's not as easy to digest, so there are always trade-offs.

Additional Exercises

1. Suggested by Tait Stevens: in Scrabble, there are limited numbers of each letter, making some words impossible to play. For example, there is only one *K*, so *KINKIER* can never be played. (We are leaving the blank tiles out of this for simplicity.) Modify your solution so that such "impossible" words are excluded from your word list. You can find the letter distribution of the game at http://en.wikipedia.org/wiki/Scrabble_letter_values.

2. Create a memory-friendly solution that works with one stem at a time. Running time can be lengthy.

3. Draw out the bit transformations in the middle of Dennis's solution. (Hint: It's easier to see if you convert the hex constants to bitwise constants.)

Answer 6

From page 17

Regexp.build()

The first thing to consider in this quiz is what does a Regexp to match a number look like? Here's the most basic answer to match 1..12:

1|2|3|4|5|6|7|8|9|10|11|12

Note that you might want to reverse the order of that, unless you can count on your anchoring to match the right thing.

Obviously, the previous works and is dirt simple to implement. Here's a submitted solution by Tanaka Akira that does pretty much that:

```
code/regex_build/limited.rb
def Regexp.build(*args)
  args = args.map {|arg| Array(arg) }.flatten.uniq.sort
  neg, pos = args.partition {|arg| arg < 0 }
  / \A (?: -0*#{Regexp.union(*neg.map {|arg| (-arg).to_s })} |
           0*#{Regexp.union(*pos.map {|arg| arg.to_s })} ) \z /x
end
```

The first line of that method is pretty clever, calling Array() on all the passed arguments. That turns Range objects into the Array equivalent and wraps simple Integers in an Array of their own. Following that up with flatten() yields a single Array of all the elements we're trying to match.

The second line just separates the arguments into positive and negative groups. Finally, the third line builds a Regexp object from the created groups using the nifty Regexp.union().

This solution handles negative numbers and allows for arbitrary leading zeros.

Is this quiz really this easy to solve? Obviously it can be, for some data sets. However, Tanaka's solution has limits. On my box, it takes only

Regexp.build(1..10_000)[29] to get a "...regular expression too big..." error. Clearly, if your data set is big, you'll need to dig a little deeper.

Shrinking a Regexp

That gets us back to our original question, but now with a qualification: What's a short way to match a number with a Regexp? The most obvious optimization to apply to our patterns is to use character classes. Returning to our 1..12 example, that might give us something like this:

```
\d|1[0-2]
```

That's getting a lot more reasonable. Going to a serious example, even 1..1_000_000 is only the following:

```
[1-9]|[1-9]\d|[1-9]\d\d|[1-9]\d\d\d|[1-9]\d\d\d\d|[1-9]\d\d\d\d\d|1000000
```

Technically, we could keep going and get to something like this:

```
[1-9]\d{0,5}|1000000
```

However, none of these solutions goes quite that far.

The main trick to building character classes is to break down the Range objects passed in. You could also lump in the individual Integer arguments, but these are pretty insignificant. One way to handle this is to add a method to the Range class to convert them into Regexp objects.

Adding a Regexp.build() over that is trivial. Here's a nice example from Mark Hubbart:

```
code/regex_build/grouped.rb
def Regexp.build(*args)
  ranges, numbers = args.partition{|item| Range === item}
  re = ranges.map{|r| r.to_re } + numbers.map{|n| /0*#{n}/ }
  /^#{Regexp.union(*re)}$/
end

class Range
  def to_re
    # normalize the range format; we want end inclusive, integer ranges
    # this part passes the load off to a newly built range if needed.
    if exclude_end?
      return( (first.to_i..last.to_i - 1).to_re )
    elsif ! (first + last).kind_of?(Integer)
      return( (first.to_i .. last.to_i).to_re )
    end
```

---

[29]Note that Ruby allows the use of _ characters in numeric literals, so you can make them more readable. The extra characters have no effect on the resulting value.

```ruby
# Deal with ranges that are wholly or partially negative. If range is
# only partially negative, split in half and get two regexen. join them
# together for the finish. If the range is wholly negative, make it
# positive, and then add a negative sign to the regexp
if first < 0 and last < 0
  # return a negatized version of the Regexp
  return /-#{(-last..-first).to_re}/
elsif first < 0
  neg = (first..-1).to_re
  pos = (0..last).to_re
  return /(?:#{neg}|#{pos})/
end

### First, create an array of new ranges that are more
### suited to regex conversion.

# a and z will be the remainders of the endpoints of the range
# as we slice it
a, z = first, last

# build the first part of the list of new ranges.
list1 = []
num = first
until num > z
  a = num # recycle the value
  # get the first power of ten that leaves a remainder
  v = 10
  v *= 10 while num % v == 0 and num != 0
  # compute the next value up
  num += v - num % v
  # store the value unless it's too high
  list1 << (a..num-1) unless num > z
end

# build the second part of the list; counting down.
list2 = []
num = last + 1
until num < a
  z = num - 1 # recycle the value
  # slice to the nearest power of ten
  v = 10
  v *= 10 while num % v == 0 and num != 0
  # compute the next value down
  num -= num % v
  # store the value if it fits
  list2 << (num..z) unless num < a
end
# get the chewy center part, if needed
center = a < z ? [a..z] : []
# our new list
```

```
    list = list1 + center + list2.reverse

    ### Next, convert each range to a Regexp.
    list.map! do |rng|
      a, z = rng.first.to_s, rng.last.to_s
      a.split(//).zip(z.split(//)).map do |(f,l)|
        case
          when f == l then f
          when f.to_i + 1 == l.to_i then "[%s%s]" % [f,l]
          when f+l == "09" then "\\d"
          else
            "[%s-%s]" % [f,l]
        end
      end.join # returns the Regexp for *that* range
    end


    ### Last, return the final Regexp
    /0*#{ list.join("|") }/
  end
end
```

The first third of the to_re() method just deals with normalizing Range objects and is very well commented.

The middle third divides the Range into Regexp-friendly chunks, which are groups that share the same number of digits. For example, here is what to_re() builds into the local list variable for 1..1_000:

```
1..9
10..99
100..999
1000..1000
```

Of course, the expression may not always break on such clean powers of ten. To give another example, 1_234..56_789 populates list with this:

```
1234..1239
1240..1299
1300..1999
2000..9999
10000..49999
50000..55999
56000..56699
56700..56789
```

The final third of to_re() builds character classes from these grouped Range objects. The code inside list.map! do ... end is pretty clever, and I recommend working through it until you can follow how it works.

This solution does not handle arbitrary leading zeros, and it is anchored at the beginning and end of a line. Negative numbers are supported.

Speeding Up the Build

Let's look at one final solution. This is similar to Mark Hubbart's approach, but as we'll see later, it's mighty quick. Here's Thomas Leitner's code:

```
code/regex_build/fast.rb
class Integer
  def to_rstr
    "#{self}"
  end
end

class Regexp
  def self.build( *args )
    Regexp.new("^(?:" + args.collect {|a| a.to_rstr}.flatten.uniq.join('|') + ")$")
  end
end

class Range
  def get_regexps( a, b, negative = false )
    arr = [a]

    af = (a == 0 ? 1.0 : a.to_f)
    bf = (b == 0 ? 1.0 : b.to_f)
    1.upto( b.to_s.length-1 ) do |i|
      pot = 10**i
      num = (af/pot).ceil*(pot) # next higher number with i zeros
      arr.insert( i,  num ) if num < b
      num = (bf/pot).floor*(pot) # next lower number with i zeros
      arr.insert( -i, num )
    end
    arr.uniq!
    arr.push( b+1 ) # +1 -> to handle it in the same way as the other elements

    result = []
    0.upto( arr.length - 2 ) do |i|
      first = arr[i].to_s
      second = (arr[i+1] - 1).to_s
      str = ''
      0.upto( first.length-1 ) do |j|
        if first[j] == second[j]
          str << first[j]
        else
          str << "[#{first[j].chr}-#{second[j].chr}]"
        end
      end
      result << str
    end

    result = result.join('|')
```

> **Lifting the Anchor**
>
> Another possibility, not explored by these solutions, is to not anchor returned expressions. This permits callers of Regexp.build() to add captures, anchoring, and even join expressions with Regexp.union() as needed. The downside of this approach would be that improperly anchored expressions might not match as intended. It gives callers more flexibility, in exchange for a little more maintenance.

```ruby
    result = "-(?:#{result})" if negative
    result
  end

  def to_rstr
    if first < 0 && last < 0
      get_regexps( -last, -first, true )
    elsif first < 0
      get_regexps( 1, -first, true ) + "|" + get_regexps( 0, last )
    else
      get_regexps( first, last )
    end
  end
end
```

Again, this is similar to Mark Hubbart's approach. The main work happens in get_regexps(). The first upto() in that method divides the numbers by multiples of ten, included in the Range. For example, the Range1..1_000_000 will fill the variable arr with the following:

```
[0, 10, 100, 1000, 10000, 100000, 1000000, 1000001]
```

The second upto() assembles the Regexp character classes for the digit sets in arr. The end result of the code is nearly identical to the last solution, but since it tracks less information as it works and makes some clever use of math to find the boundaries, it works a touch quicker.

The previous solution does not allow leading zeros, and it captures nothing. Negative numbers are supported. The returned Regexp is also anchored at the beginning and end of a line, so it must match the entire number.

Timing the Solutions

A big part of using these solutions is a question of how long you'll have to wait for a Regexp object to be built and how quickly the result can find a match. Here are some benchmarks for build times:

	user	system	total	real
Tanaka Akira	26.370000	0.150000	26.520000	(26.624490)
Mark Hubbart	9.890000	0.040000	9.930000	(9.944374)
Thomas Leitner	5.270000	0.030000	5.300000	(5.323440)

These were computed with the following code:

`code/regex_build/build_times.rb`

```ruby
#!/usr/local/bin/ruby
require "benchmark"


Benchmark.bm(16) do |stats|
  { "Mark Hubbart"   => "grouped",
    "Thomas Leitner" => "fast",
    "Tanaka Akira"   => "limited" }.each do |name, library|
    require library
    stats.report(name) do
      50_000.times { Regexp.build(1, 2, 5..100) }
    end
  end
end
```

Finally, here are some matching benchmarks (build times excluded from results):

	user	system	total	real
Tanaka Akira	19.090000	0.040000	19.130000	(19.151167)
Mark Hubbart	0.100000	0.000000	0.100000	(0.105672)
Thomas Leitner	0.100000	0.000000	0.100000	(0.098846)

Again, here is the code:

`code/regex_build/match_times.rb`

```ruby
#!/usr/local/bin/ruby
require "benchmark"


Benchmark.bm(16) do |stats|
  { "Mark Hubbart"   => "grouped",
    "Thomas Leitner" => "fast",
    "Tanaka Akira"   => "limited" }.each do |name, library|
    require library
    regex = Regexp.build(1..5_000)
    stats.report(name) do
      50_000.times { "4098" =~ regex }
    end
  end
end
```

Additional Exercises

1. Come up with an algorithm that reduces Regexps down to a super small representation, like [1-9]\d{0,5}|1000000 for 1..1_000_000.

2. Use the benchmark library on the compact algorithm from the previous exercise and on your original solution, as well as those shown in this quiz. How does it compare?

3. Adapt your solution to handle non-Integer input, so you could call it like Regexp.build("cat", "bat", "rat", "dog").

HighLine

The solutions to this quiz came in all shapes and sizes. That's great, because it helped us see what kind of functionality people really wanted out of a library such as this.

Implementations were equally varied. Some people wrote procedural code, just building the needed methods and injecting them into Kernel so they would be globally available. Others presented their solution as a framework of classes.

A Class-Based Solution

Ryan Leavengood's solution is class based. That allows you to assign the input and output streams, for working with sockets perhaps. It also adds an object construction step, though as a trade-off. The listing starts on the next page.

We can see that the code starts by adding a helper method to String. When called, that method ensures that the String ends in a space. If it doesn't, it returns another String that does.

Right at the beginning of HighLine, you can see the input and output stream handling setup that I mentioned earlier. These streams default to $stdout and $stdin for console output, but there's no reason you couldn't set them to a File stream or Socket.

Next up is the main interface, the ask() method. The method starts by appending a default to the question (for display), if a default is given. Then we launch into some kind of a validation_loop() that seems to be checking for an answer or the case that one is not given when a default is allowed. The method ends by returning the answer or a default.

```
code/highline/highline-oo.rb
class String
  def pad_if_needed
    self[-1].chr != ' ' ? self + ' ' : self
  end
end

class HighLine
  attr_accessor :io_out, :io_in
  def initialize(io_out=$stdout, io_in=$stdin)
    @io_out, @io_in = io_out, io_in
  end

  def ask(question, default=nil)
    q = question.pad_if_needed
    q += "[#{default}] " if default
    answer = validation_loop(q) do |input|
      input.size > 0 or default
    end
    answer.size > 0 ? answer : default
  end

  def ask_if?(question)
    answer = validation_loop(question.pad_if_needed+'(y,n) ') do |input|
      %w(y n yes no).include?(input.downcase)
    end
    answer.downcase[0,1] == 'y'
  end

  def ask_int(question, range=nil)
    validation_loop(question) do |input|
      input =~ /\A\s*-?\d+\s*\Z/ and (not range or range.member?(input.to_i))
    end.to_i
  end

  def ask_float(question, range=nil)
    validation_loop(question) do |input|
      input =~ /\A\s*-?\d+(.\d*)?\s*\Z/ and
        (not range or range.member?(input.to_f))
    end.to_f
  end

  def header(title)
    dashes = '-'*(title.length+4)
    io_out.puts(dashes)
    io_out.puts("| #{title} |")
    io_out.puts(dashes)
  end

  def list(items, prompt=nil)
    items.each_with_index do |item, i|
```

```
      @io_out.puts "#{i+1}. #{item}"
    end
    valid_range = 1..items.length
    prompt = "Please make a selection: " unless prompt
    answer = validation_loop(prompt) do |input|
      valid_range.member?(input.to_i)
    end
    # Though the list is shown using a 1-indexed list, return 0-indexed
    return answer.to_i-1
  end

  def validation_loop(prompt)
    loop do
      @io_out.print prompt.pad_if_needed
      answer = @io_in.gets
      if answer
        answer.chomp!
        if yield answer
          return answer
        end
      end
    end
  end
end
```

Skip down now, and examine the validation_loop(). This method handles the stream I/O. It begins by writing out the provided prompt. Then an answer is read from the input stream, chomp()ed, and checked against the provided block. If the block OKs the answer, it's returned. Otherwise, the whole process loop()s until a valid answer is found.

From there, ask_if(), ask_int(), and ask_float() are trivial to understand. All three are similar to ask(), except they are looking for their specific input format and then doing the conversion before returning.

The next method, header(), is just a helper that draws an ASCII border around the provided title. Clever idea, though. I can even see taking it a step further to draw things like tables.

Finally, list() adds a great concept not considered by the quiz specification. With it, users can display simple menus for users to choose an option from. You pass the items to display and the desired prompt. From there, list() numbers them, displays them, retrieves a valid choice, and returns the index of the choice made. That greatly simplifies a common task in command-line applications.

Testing I/O

The rest of Ryan's code is the unit tests:

```
code/highline/highline-oo.rb
# Unit Tests
if $0 == __FILE__
  class MockIO
    attr_accessor :output, :input

    def initialize
      reset
    end

    def reset
      @index = 0
      @input=nil
      @output=''
    end

    def print(*a)
      @output << a.join('')
    end

    def puts(*a)
      if a.size > 1
        @output << a.join("\n")
      else
        @output << a[0] << "\n"
      end
    end

    def gets
      if @input.kind_of?(Array)
        @index += 1
        @input[@index-1]
      else
        @input
      end
    end
  end

  require 'test/unit'

  class TC_HighLine < Test::Unit::TestCase
    def initialize(name)
      super(name)
      @mock_io = MockIO.new
      @highline = HighLine.new(@mock_io, @mock_io)
    end
```

```ruby
def setup
  @mock_io.reset
end

def test_ask
  question = 'Am I the coolest?'
  @mock_io.input = [nil, '', "\n", "yes\n"]
  assert_equal(@mock_io.input[-1].chomp, @highline.ask(question))
  assert_equal((question+' ')*4, @mock_io.output)
end

def test_ask_default
  question = 'Where are you from? '
  default = 'Florida'
  @mock_io.input = [nil, "\n"]
  assert_equal(default, @highline.ask(question, default))
  assert_equal((question+"[#{default}] ")*2, @mock_io.output)
end

def test_ask_if
  question = 'Is Ruby the best programming language? '
  @mock_io.input = [nil, "0\n", "blah\n", "YES\n"]
  assert_equal(true, @highline.ask_if?(question))
  assert_equal((question+' (y,n) ')*4, @mock_io.output)
end

def test_ask_int
  question = 'Give me a number:'
  @mock_io.input = [nil, '', "\n", ' ', "blah\n", "  -4  \n"]
  assert_equal(-4, @highline.ask_int(question))
  assert_equal((question+' ')*6, @mock_io.output)
  @mock_io.reset
  @mock_io.input = [nil, '', "\n", ' ', "blah\n", "3604\n"]
  assert_equal(3604, @highline.ask_int(question))
  assert_equal((question+' ')*6, @mock_io.output)
end

def test_ask_int_range
  question = 'How old are you?'
  @mock_io.input = [nil, '', "\n", ' ', "blah\n", "106\n", "28\n"]
  assert_equal(28, @highline.ask_int(question, 0..105))
  assert_equal((question+' ')*7, @mock_io.output)
end

def test_ask_float
  question = 'Give me a floating point number:'
  @mock_io.input = [nil, '', "\n", ' ', "blah\n", "  -4.3  \n"]
  assert_equal(-4.3, @highline.ask_float(question))
  assert_equal((question+' ')*6, @mock_io.output)
  @mock_io.reset
  @mock_io.input = [nil, '', "\n", ' ', "blah\n", "560\n"]
```

```
        assert_equal(560.0, @highline.ask_float(question))
        assert_equal((question+' ')*6, @mock_io.output)
    end

    def test_ask_float_range
        question = 'Give me a floating point number between 5.0 and 13.5:'
        @mock_io.input = [ nil, '', "\n", ' ', "blah\n", "  -4.3   \n", "4.9\n",
                          "13.6\n", "7.55\n" ]
        assert_equal(7.55, @highline.ask_float(question, 5.0..13.5))
        assert_equal((question+' ')*9, @mock_io.output)
    end

    def test_header
        title = 'HighLine Manual'
        @highline.header(title)
        output = "-------------\n| HighLine Manual |\n-------------\n"
        assert_equal(output, @mock_io.output)
    end

    def test_list
        items = ['Ruby','Python','Perl']
        prompt = 'Please choose your favorite programming language: '
        @mock_io.input = [nil, "0\n", "blah\n", "4\n", "1\n"]
        assert_equal(0, @highline.list(items, prompt))
        assert_equal("1. Ruby\n2. Python\n3. Perl\n#{prompt * 5}",
                    @mock_io.output)
    end
  end
end
```

Those tests show off usage well, so you can see how this library works. You can also see that Ryan builds a MockIO object to make it possible to test the library. Ryan can pass this object supporting the needed methods from IO into his HighLine framework and later query the object about what would have been output, had an actual IO object been used. This is a powerful testing technique even for complex applications. The end result is a helpful and proven library for console input and output management.

The Official HighLine

My own solution walked the line between procedures and classes. It had a complete object-oriented design but allowed you to import some methods into the global namespace for convenience. Let's see how something like that is done:

`code/highline/highline.rb`

```ruby
require "highline/answer"

class HighLine
  class QuestionError < StandardError
    # do nothing, just creating a unique error type
  end

  # Create an instance of HighLine, connected to the streams _input_
  # and _output_.
  def initialize( input = $stdin, output = $stdout )
    @input  = input
    @output = output
  end

  def ask( question, answer_type = String, &details )
    answer = Answer.new(answer_type, &details)

    say(question)
    begin
      input = fetch_line
      unless answer.valid?(input)
        explain_error( question,
                       answer.responses[:not_valid],
                       answer.ask_on_error )
        raise QuestionError
      end
      result = answer.convert(input)
      if answer.accept?(result)
        result
      else
        explain_error( question,
                       answer.responses[:failed_tests],
                       answer.ask_on_error )
        raise QuestionError
      end
    rescue QuestionError
      retry
    rescue ArgumentError
      explain_error( question,
                     answer.responses[:invalid_type],
                     answer.ask_on_error )
      retry
    rescue NameError
      explain_error( question,
                     answer.responses[:ambiguous_completion],
                     answer.ask_on_error )
      retry
    end
  end
end
```

We're looking at the heart of HighLine here, the ask() method. Before we get to that, though, we can see that HighLine pulls in another source file, which we will meet in a bit. It also declares a unique type of error for internal use. Then you can see that initialize() is just for assigning streams, which default to $stdin and $stdout.

The ask() method looks more complicated than it is. Most of it is just error handling. First, an Answer object is constructed from the requested answer_type and a given block. That's the object from the other source file, and we will examine it in a bit. From there the code grabs input from the user with fetch_line(). Then it uses a three-step process to valid?()ate the answer, convert() it, and accept?() it. Again, we will see those methods when we get to the other class. When something goes wrong in here, we can see errors being thrown. It seems that an explanation is sent to the user, and then **retry** causes Ruby to try the question again so we can get a valid answer.

Here's all the non-Answer methods we saw being called in there:

```
code/highline/highline.rb
class HighLine
  def agree( yes_or_no_question )
    ask(yes_or_no_question, proc { |a| a =~ /\AY(?:es)?\Z/i ? true : false })
  end

  def say( statement )
    if statement[-1, 1] == " " or statement[-1, 1] == "\t"
      @output.print(statement)
      @output.flush
    else
      @output.puts(statement)
    end
  end

  private

  def explain_error( question, error, reask )
    say(error)
    if reask == :question
      say(question)
    elsif reask
      say(reask)
    end
  end

  def fetch_line(  )
    @input.gets.chomp
  end
end
```

There should be very few surprises in there. agree() is just ask_if() from the quiz example. say() is used to print messages for the user to see. The only trick there is that lines ending in whitespace use print() and flush() instead of puts(). That allows you to ask "Age?" and read the answer from the same line. explain_error() just forwards the problem message to the user and then prompts them with a follow-up question. fetch_line() reads lines from the keyboard.

Let's get to that Answer object now:

`code/highline/highline/answer.rb`

```ruby
#!/usr/local/bin/ruby -w

require "optparse"
require "date"

class HighLine
  class Answer
    # Create an instance of HighLine::Answer.
    def initialize( type )
      @type = type

      @ask_on_error = "?   "
      @member       = nil
      @validate     = nil
      @responses    = Hash.new

      yield self if block_given?

      @responses = { :ambiguous_completion =>
                       "Ambiguous choice.   " +
                       "Please choose one of #{@type.inspect}.",
                     :failed_tests         =>
                       "Your answer must be a member of " +
                       "#{@member.inspect}.",
                     :invalid_type         =>
                       "You must enter a valid #{@type}.",
                     :not_valid            =>
                       "Your answer isn't valid " +
                       "(#{@validate.inspect}).' " }.merge(@responses)
    end

    attr_accessor :ask_on_error, :member, :validate
    attr_reader :responses

    def convert( string )
      if @type.nil?
        string
      elsif [Float, Integer, String].include?(@type)
        Kernel.send(@type.to_s.to_sym, string)
```

```
          elsif @type == Symbol
            string.to_sym
          elsif @type == Regexp
            Regexp.new(string)
          elsif @type.is_a?(Array)
            @type.extend(OptionParser::Completion)
            @type.complete(string).last
          elsif [Date, DateTime].include?(@type)
            @type.parse(string)
          elsif @type.is_a?(Proc)
            @type[string]
          end
        end

        def accept?( answer_object )
          @member.nil? or @member.member?(answer_object)
        end

        def valid?( string )
          @validate.nil? or string =~ @validate
        end
      end
    end
end
```

This is really just a data class. It sets a bunch of defaults and then allows the user to change them to fit their needs by passing the object to a block in initialize(). Inside the block, the user can use the accessors to set details for the answer they are after.

The only method really worth discussing here is convert(). You can see that it supports many types the answer can be converted into including Integer, Symbol, or even DateTime. This method can do two interesting forms of conversion. First, if the @type (answer_type from the HighLine layer) is set to an Array of values, the method will autocomplete the user's answer to a matching value, using code borrowed from Option-Parser. Finally, if you set @type to a Proc object, it will be called to handle whatever custom conversion you need. Glance back at HighLine.agree() if you want to see an example.

So far, we've seen the class system, which could be used directly via require "highline" when needed. Most of the time, though, we would probably prefer global access to these methods. For that, HighLine provides another file you could load with require "highline/import":

```
code/highline/highline/import.rb
#!/usr/local/bin/ruby -w

require "highline"
require "forwardable"

$terminal = HighLine.new

module Kernel
  extend Forwardable
  def_delegators :$terminal, :agree, :ask, :say
end
```

The idea here is that we can stick a HighLine object in a global variable and then just modify Kernel to delegate bare agree(), ask(), or say() calls to that object. The standard library, Forwardable, handles the latter part of that process for us via def_delegators(). You just give it the name of the object to handle the calls and a list of methods to forward. Notice that Kernel needs to extend Forwardable to gain access to def_delegators().

This library proved helpful enough to me that I continued to develop it and made it available to the Ruby community through RubyForge. HighLine has grown and matured from the original quiz submission and now supports many, many features. Recently, a second developer, Greg Brown, signed on, bringing a comprehensive menu framework to the project. If you would like to play with the library, see http://highline.rubyforge.org/ for instructions on obtaining the latest release.

Additional Exercises

1. Create the ASCII table feature mentioned in the discussion of Ryan's header() method.

2. Work up a patch to add this feature to the HighLine library on Ruby-Forge.

3. Extend your solution to fetch an entire Array of answers from the user.

Answer 8

From page 21

Roman Numerals

Solving this quiz is easy, but how easy? Well, the problem gives us the conversion chart, which is just crying out to be a Hash:

```
code/roman_numerals/simple.rb
ROMAN_MAP = { 1    => "I",
              4    => "IV",
              5    => "V",
              9    => "IX",
              10   => "X",
              40   => "XL",
              50   => "L",
              90   => "XC",
              100  => "C",
              400  => "CD",
              500  => "D",
              900  => "CM",
              1000 => "M" }
```

That's the version from my code, but most solutions used something very similar.

From there we just need to_roman() and to_arabic() methods, right? Sounded like too much work for a lazy bum like me, so I cheated. If you build a conversion table, you can get away with just doing the conversion one way:

```
code/roman_numerals/simple.rb
ROMAN_NUMERALS = Array.new(3999) do |index|
  target = index + 1
  ROMAN_MAP.keys.sort { |a, b| b <=> a }.inject("") do |roman, div|
    times, target = target.divmod(div)
    roman << ROMAN_MAP[div] * times
  end
end
```

This is the to_roman() method many solutions hit on. I just used mine to fill an Array. The algorithm here isn't too tough. Divide the target number by each value there is a Roman numeral for copy the numeral that many times reduce the target, and repeat. Ruby's divmod() is great for this.

From there, it's trivial to wrap a Unix filter around the Array. However, I do like to validate input, so I did one more little prep task:

code/roman_numerals/simple.rb
```
IS_ROMAN = / ^ M{0,3}
                (?:CM|DC{0,3}|CD|C{0,3})
                (?:XC|LX{0,3}|XL|X{0,3})
                (?:IX|VI{0,3}|IV|I{0,3}) $ /ix
IS_ARABIC = /^(?:[123]\d{3}|[1-9]\d{0,2})$/
```

That first Regexp is a validator for the Roman letter combinations we accept, split up by powers of ten. The second Regexp is a pattern to match 1..3999, a number in the range we can convert to and from.

Now, we're ready for the Unix filter wrapper:

code/roman_numerals/simple.rb
```
if __FILE__ == $0
  ARGF.each_line() do |line|
    line.chomp!
    case line
    when IS_ROMAN  then puts ROMAN_NUMERALS.index(line) + 1
    when IS_ARABIC then puts ROMAN_NUMERALS[line.to_i - 1]
    else raise "Invalid input:  #{line}"
    end
  end
end
```

In English that says, for each line of input, see whether it matches IS_ROMAN, and if it does, look it up in the Array. If it doesn't match IS_ROMAN but does match IS_ARABIC, index into the Array to get the match. If none of that is true, complain about the broken input.

Saving Some Memory

If you don't want to build the Array, you just need to create the other converter. It's not hard. J E Bailey's script did both, so let's look at that:

`code/roman_numerals/dual_conversions.rb`

```ruby
#!/usr/bin/env ruby

@data = [
[ "M"  , 1000],
[ "CM" , 900],
[ "D"  , 500],
[ "CD" , 400],
[ "C"  , 100],
[ "XC" , 90],
[ "L"  , 50],
[ "XL" , 40],
[ "X"  , 10],
[ "IX" ,  9],
[ "V"  ,  5],
[ "IV" ,  4],
[ "I"  ,  1]
]

@roman = %r{^[CDILMVX]*$}
@arabic = %r{^[0-9]*$}

def to_roman(num)
  reply = ""
  for key, value in @data
    count, num = num.divmod(value)
    reply << (key * count)
  end
  reply
end

def to_arabic(rom)
  reply = 0
  for key, value in @data
    while rom.index(key) == 0
      reply += value
      rom.slice!(key)
    end
  end
  reply
end

$stdin.each do |line|
  case line
  when @roman
    puts to_arabic(line)
  when @arabic
    puts to_roman(line.to_i)
  end
end
```

Joe Asks...
toRoman() or to_roman()?

The methods in J E's solution were originally toRoman() and toArabic(). These method names use an unusual (in Ruby circles) naming convention often referred to as *camelCase*. Typical Ruby style is to name methods and variables in *snake_case* (such as to_roman() and to_arabic()). We do typically use a variant of the former (with a capital first letter) in the names of classes and modules, though.

Why is this important?

Well, with any language first you need to learn the grammar, but eventually you want to know the slang, right? Same thing. Someday you may want to write Ruby the way that Ruby gurus do.

I told you we all used something similar to my Hash. Here it's just an Array of tuples.

Right below that, you'll see J E's data identifying Regexp declarations. They're not as exact as my versions, but certainly they are easier on the eyes.

Next we see a to_roman() method, which looks very familiar. The implementation is almost identical to mine, but it comes out a little cleaner here since it isn't used to load an Array.

Then we reach the method of interest, to_arabic(). The method starts by setting a reply variable to *0*. Then it hunts for each Roman numeral in the rom String, increments reply by that value, and removes that numeral from the String. The ordering of the @data Array ensures that an *XL* or *IV* will be found before an *X* or *I*.

Finally, the code provides the quiz-specified Unix filter behavior. Again, this is very similar to my own solution, but with conversion routines going both ways.

Romanizing Ruby

Those are simple solutions, but let's jump over to Dave Burt's code for a little Ruby voodoo. Dave's code builds a module, RomanNumerals, with to_integer() and from_integer(), similar to what we've discussed previously. The module also defines is_roman_numeral?() for checking exactly what the name claims and some helpful constants such as DIGITS, MAX, and REGEXP.

`code/roman_numerals/roman_numerals.rb`

```ruby
# Contains methods to convert integers to Roman numeral strings, and vice versa.
module RomanNumerals

  # Maps Roman numeral digits to their integer values
  DIGITS = {
    'I' => 1,
    'V' => 5,
    'X' => 10,
    'L' => 50,
    'C' => 100,
    'D' => 500,
    'M' => 1000
  }

  # The largest integer representable as a Roman numerable by this module
  MAX = 3999

  # Maps some integers to their Roman numeral values
  @@digits_lookup = DIGITS.inject({
    4 => 'IV',
    9 => 'IX',
    40 => 'XL',
    90 => 'XC',
    400 => 'CD',
    900 => 'CM'}) do |memo, pair|
    memo.update({pair.last => pair.first})
  end

  # Based on Regular Expression Grabbag in the O'Reilly Perl Cookbook, #6.23
  REGEXP = /^M*(D?C{0,3}|C[DM])(L?X{0,3}|X[LC])(V?I{0,3}|I[VX])$/i

  # Converts +int+ to a Roman numeral
  def self.from_integer(int)
    return nil if int < 0 || int > MAX
    remainder = int
    result = ''
    @@digits_lookup.keys.sort.reverse.each do |digit_value|
      while remainder >= digit_value
        remainder -= digit_value
        result += @@digits_lookup[digit_value]
      end
      break if remainder <= 0
    end
    result
  end
```

```
# Converts +roman_string+, a Roman numeral, to an integer
def self.to_integer(roman_string)
  return nil unless roman_string.is_roman_numeral?
  last = nil
  roman_string.to_s.upcase.split(//).reverse.inject(0) do |memo, digit|
    if digit_value = DIGITS[digit]
      if last && last > digit_value
        memo -= digit_value
      else
        memo += digit_value
      end
      last = digit_value
    end
    memo
  end
end

# Returns true if +string+ is a Roman numeral.
def self.is_roman_numeral?(string)
  REGEXP =~ string
end
end
```

I doubt we need to go over that code again, but I do want to point out one clever point. Notice how Dave uses a neat dance to keep things like *IV* out of DIGITS. In doing so, we see the unusual construct memo.update({pair.last => pair.first}), instead of the seemingly more natural memo[pair.last] = pair.first. The reason is that the former returns the Hash itself, satisfying the continuous update cycle of inject().

Anyway, the module is a small chunk of Dave's code, and the rest is fun. Let's see him put it to use:

code/roman_numerals/roman_numerals.rb

```
class String
  # Considers string a Roman numeral,
  # and converts it to the corresponding integer.
  def to_i_roman
    RomanNumerals.to_integer(self)
  end
  # Returns true if the subject is a Roman numeral.
  def is_roman_numeral?
    RomanNumerals.is_roman_numeral?(self)
  end
end
class Integer
  # Converts this integer to a Roman numeral.
  def to_s_roman
    RomanNumerals.from_integer(self) || ''
  end
end
```

First, he adds converters to String and Integer. This allows you to code things such as the following:

```
puts "In the year #{1999.to_s_roman} ..."
```

Fun, but there's more. For Dave's final magic trick he defines a class:

code/roman_numerals/roman_numerals.rb

```ruby
# Integers that look like Roman numerals
class RomanNumeral
  attr_reader :to_s, :to_i

  @@all_roman_numerals = []

  # May be initialized with either a string or an integer
  def initialize(value)
    case value
    when Integer
      @to_s = value.to_s_roman
      @to_i = value
    else
      @to_s = value.to_s
      @to_i = value.to_s.to_i_roman
    end
    @@all_roman_numerals[to_i] = self
  end

  # Factory method: returns an equivalent existing object if such exists,
  # or a new one
  def self.get(value)
    if value.is_a?(Integer)
      to_i = value
    else
      to_i = value.to_s.to_i_roman
    end
    @@all_roman_numerals[to_i] || RomanNumeral.new(to_i)
  end

  def inspect
    to_s
  end

  # Delegates missing methods to Integer, converting arguments to Integer,
  # and converting results back to RomanNumeral
  def method_missing(sym, *args)
    unless to_i.respond_to?(sym)
      raise NoMethodError.new(
        "undefined method '#{sym}' for #{self}:#{self.class}")
    end
    result = to_i.send(sym,
      *args.map {|arg| arg.is_a?(RomanNumeral) ? arg.to_i : arg })
    case result
```

```
      when Integer
        RomanNumeral.get(result)
      when Enumerable
        result.map do |element|
          element.is_a?(Integer) ? RomanNumeral.get(element) : element
        end
      else
        result
      end
    end
  end
end
```

If you use the factory method get() to create these objects, it's efficient with reuse, always giving you the same object for the same value.

Note that method_missing() basically delegates to Integer at the end, so you can treat these objects mostly as Integer objects. This class allows you to code things like thus:

```
IV = RomanNumeral.get(4)
IV + 5 # => IX
```

Even better, though, is that Dave removes the need for that first step with the following:

`code/roman_numerals/roman_numerals.rb`

```
# Enables uppercase Roman numerals to be used interchangeably with integers.
# They are autovivified RomanNumeral constants
# Synopsis:
#    4 + IV          #=> VIII
#    VIII + 7        #=> XV
#    III ** III      #=> XXVII
#    VIII.divmod(III) #=> [II, II]
def Object.const_missing sym
  unless RomanNumerals::REGEXP === sym.to_s
    raise NameError.new("uninitialized constant: #{sym}")
  end
  const_set(sym, RomanNumeral.get(sym))
end
```

This makes it so that Ruby will automatically turn constants like IX into RomanNumeral objects as needed. That's just smooth.

Finally, the listing at the top of the facing page shows Dave's actual solution to the quiz using the previous tools:

`code/roman_numerals/roman_numerals.rb`

```ruby
# Quiz solution: filter that swaps Roman and arabic numbers
if __FILE__ == $0
  ARGF.each do |line|
    line.chomp!
    if line.is_roman_numeral?
      puts line.to_i_roman
    else
      puts line.to_i.to_s_roman
    end
  end
end
```

Additional Exercises

1. Modify your solution to scan free-flowing text documents, replacing all valid Roman numerals with their Arabic equivalents.

2. Create a solution that maps out the conversions similar to the first example in this discussion, but do it without using a 4,000-element Array kept in memory.

Rock Paper Scissors

This quiz is a classic computer science problem, though it is often done with a different game.

The game chosen doesn't much matter, but the idea is that there really shouldn't be much strategy involved. For the game of Rock Paper Scissors, the winning strategy is to be purely random, as Benedikt Huber explained on the Ruby Talk mailing list:[30]

> You can't give any predictions on the next move of a random player. Therefore, you have a 1/3 probability to choose a winning, losing, or drawing move.

To be fair, Rock Paper Scissors does have quite a bit of strategy theory these days, but the conditions of that theory (mostly body language) are unavailable to computer players. Entire books have been written on the subject, believe it or not.[31]

So, is random the best we can do? Is that hard to build? Uh, no. Here's a sample by Avi Bryant:

```
code/rock_paper_scissors/abj_players.rb
class AJBRandomPlayer < Player
  def choose
    [:paper, :scissors, :rock][rand(3)]
  end
end
```

---

[30]Ruby Quiz is hosted on the Ruby Talk mailing list, and you will often see discussion there about the problems. You can find more information about this mailing list for general Ruby discussion at http://www.ruby-lang.org/en/20020104.html.

[31]http://www.worldrps.com/

If we test that, we get the expected 50/50 results:

```
AJBRandomPlayer vs. JEGPaperPlayer
                AJBRandomPlayer: 511.0
                JEGPaperPlayer: 489.0
                AJBRandomPlayer Wins
AJBRandomPlayer vs. JEGQueuePlayer
                AJBRandomPlayer: 499.5
                JEGQueuePlayer: 500.5
                JEGQueuePlayer Wins
```

Outthinking a Random Player

Of course, that's so uninteresting, you're probably beginning to wonder if my quiz-selecting skills are on the fritz. Possibly, but interesting solutions make me look good nonetheless. Christian Neukirchen sent in more than one of those. Look at all these great strategies:

- CNBiasInverter: Choose so that your bias will be the inverted opponent's bias.

- CNIrrflug: Pick a random choice. If you win, use it again; else, use a random choice.

- CNStepAhead: Try to think a step ahead. If you win, use the choice where you would have lost. If you lose, use the choice where you would have won. Use the same on a draw.

- CNBiasFlipper: Always use the choice that beats what the opponent chose most or second to most often.

- CNBiasBreaker: Always use the choice that beats what the opponent chose most often.

- CNMeanPlayer: Pick a random choice. If you win, use it again; else, use the opponent's choice.

I really should show all of those here, but that would make for a ridiculously large chapter. Let's go with Christian's favorite:

Spring Cleaning
I factored code out into the total() method in the hope it would be a little easier to read.

`code/rock_paper_scissors/cn_bias_inverter.rb`
```ruby
class CNBiasInverter < Player
  def initialize(opponent)
    super
    @biases = {:rock => 0, :scissors => 0, :paper => 0}
  end

  def choose
    n = ::Kernel.rand( total(:rock, :scissors, :paper) ).to_i
    case n
```

```
    when 0..@biases[:rock]
      :paper
    when @biases[:rock]..total(:rock, :scissors)
      :rock
    when total(:rock, :scissors)..total(:rock, :scissors, :paper)
      :scissors
    else
      p total(:rock, :scissors)..@biases[:paper]
      abort n.to_s
    end
  end

  def result(you, them, win_lose_or_draw)
    @biases[them] += 1
  end

  private

  def total(*biases)
    biases.inject(0) { |sum, bias| sum + @biases[bias] }
  end
end
```

initialize() sets up a Hash for tracking the biases. result() is the complement to that. It adjusts the proper bias count each time the opponent makes a selection.

choose() does all the interesting work. It chooses a random number between zero and the total of all the bias counts.[32] That number is then associated with the indicated bias by some clever use of ranges, and the opposite of that bias is returned as CNBiasInverter's choice.

In other words, as the opponent chooses more and more of a particular item, the bias count for that item climbs. This will cause the semirandom choice to drift toward the opposite of that favored move.

Let's compare with our baseline:

```
CNBiasInverter vs. JEGPaperPlayer
            CNBiasInverter: 995.0
            JEGPaperPlayer: 5.0
            CNBiasInverter Wins
CNBiasInverter vs. JEGQueuePlayer
            CNBiasInverter: 653.5
            JEGQueuePlayer: 346.5
            CNBiasInverter Wins
```

---

[32]The unusual ::Kernel.rand() call here just makes sure we are calling the rand() method defined in the Kernel module. This defensive programming technique will make more sense as we get further into the discussion....

The results are getting better. But, of course, random still wins:

```
AJBRandomPlayer vs. CNBiasInverter
                AJBRandomPlayer: 509.5
                CNBiasInverter: 490.5
                AJBRandomPlayer Wins
```

There were many, many interesting strategies, like the previous one. But random remained the great equalizer. This leads us to the critical question: what exactly is the point of this exercise?

Cheat to Win

Cheating, of course!

With a challenge like this quiz, it's common to engineer the environment to be ripe for cheating. Since there's no winning strategy available, we'll need to bend the rules a little bit.[33] That's because programmers have enormous egos and can't stand to lose at anything!

What's the ultimate cheat? Well, here's my first thought:

code/rock_paper_scissors/jeg_cheater.rb
```ruby
#!/usr/biin/env ruby

class JEGCheater < Player
  def initialize( opponent )
    Object.const_get(opponent).class_eval do
      alias_method :old_choose, :choose
      def choose
        :paper
      end
    end
  end

  def choose
    :scissors
  end
end
```

It doesn't get much easier than that! The initialize() method uses the passed-in name of the opponent to locate the correct Class object and redefine the choose() method of that Class to something super easy to deal with. The opponent is modified to always throw :paper, and JEGCheater always throws :scissors.

---

[33]Technically, it's not even cheating. The definition of *cheat* that applies here is "to violate rules dishonestly." Go back, and reread the quiz if you need to....

That's 100% successful against anything we've seen thus far. Worse, any player who goes up against JEGCheater is permanently modified, leaving you vulnerable to clever strategies like CNBiasInverter previously:

```
AJBRandomPlayer vs. JEGCheater
                AJBRandomPlayer: 0
                JEGCheater: 1000
                JEGCheater Wins
AJBRandomPlayer vs. CNBiasInverter
                AJBRandomPlayer: 4.5
                CNBiasInverter: 995.5
                CNBiasInverter Wins
JEGCheater vs. CNBiasInverter
                JEGCheater: 1000
                CNBiasInverter: 0
                JEGCheater Wins
```

Ouch!

Psychic Players

Another cheat used by more than one submitter was to try to predict an opponent's move and then respond with a counter. Here is Benedikt Huber's version:

code/rock_paper_scissors/bh_cheat_player.rb

```ruby
KILLER = { :rock => :paper, :paper => :scissors, :scissors => :rock }

class BHCheatPlayer < Player

  def initialize( opponent )
    super
    @opp = Object.const_get(opponent).new(self)
  end

  def choose
    KILLER[@opp.choose]
  end

  def result(you,them,result)
    @opp.result(them,you,result)
  end

end
```

Again initialize() retrieves the Class object, but instead of modifying the Class, it simply creates an internal copy of the opponent. result() forwards each pick to the copied opponent to keep it synchronized with the real opponent. From there, choose() is obvious: see what the opponent is about to do, and counter.

It was pointed out on Ruby Talk that this doesn't demolish random players; however, against any random strategy, this becomes a random player. Countering a random choice is a still a random move, even if the choice isn't what the opponent is about to do.

Thinking Outside the Box

There are other great cheats, and some approaches were even overlooked. For example, no one tried to modify the score, but it can be done. Next time someone tells you there's no way to get better odds than a random player, don't underestimate the power of cheating! A large part of programming is learning to attack problems from different angles until you find something that works.

Additional Exercises

1. Build a cheater that beats JEGCheater 100% of the time.

2. Build a player that repairs itself if cheater code modifies it.

3. Build a cheater that adjusts the game scores in the server.

4. Build a player that flawlessly predicts a random player's moves and uses that knowledge to win.

Answer 10
From page 29

Knight's Travails

One neat aspect of doing a simple problem now and then is checking out the elegant solutions people apply to it. With Ruby, that usually means some pretty code, at least in my mind. For this problem, I really thought Matthew D Moss wrote some code that showed off how pretty and clever Ruby can be. His solution is overflowing with cool idioms, so let's dive right in. Here's a "helper class" from the code:

Spring Cleaning

I replaced 'a'[0] and '1'[0] with the more common ?a and ?1, just to aid reader recognition.

`code/knights_travails/pretty.rb`

```ruby
class Tile
  attr_reader :x, :y
  protected   :x, :y

  def initialize(x, y)
    @x, @y = x, y
  end

  def Tile.named(s)
    Tile.new(s.downcase[0] - ?a, s[1] - ?1)
  end

  def valid?
    (0...8) === @x and (0...8) === @y
  end

  def to_s
    to_str
  end

  def to_str
    %w(a b c d e f g h)[@x] + %w(1 2 3 4 5 6 7 8)[@y] if valid?
  end

  def ==(c)
    @x == c.x and @y == c.y
  end
```

```
def adjacent?(c)
  dx = (@x - c.x).abs
  dy = (@y - c.y).abs
  valid? and c.valid? and (dx == 1 && dy == 2 or dx == 2 && dy == 1)
end
end
```

I couldn't decide if this class was named correctly. It represents a square, or *tile*, of the chessboard, but when I think of a square, it's as a container for a piece. That's not what we're dealing with here. This class just holds *x* and *y* coordinates for the square on the board. Once you grasp that, the code is easy to follow. You can see this setup right at the top of the class with the x() and y() readers and initialize() storing the values. From there, though, the work gets interesting.

The Tile.named() method is another constructor. Instead of building a Tile from *x* and *y* coordinates ranging from 0 to 7, it builds them from traditional chess notation for a square like "a4" by converting to coordinates and calling the other constructor. The first step converts the leading letter to an index by normalizing case and subtracting the character value of *a* from the character value of the square's letter. The second conversion works the same way for the number.

The next method is valid?(). Its only job is to determine whether this is a legal square on a real chessboard. That translates to needing *x* and *y* in the Range(0..7). Note that these Ranges are actually built with the ... operator, which excludes the last number. The === check is used in conditionals for **case** statements, but you're welcome to call it yourself, as you can see. It's an alias for Range.member?(), which just checks that the argument is in the Range.

Both to_s() and to_str() allow the object to behave as a String, as long as it's a valid Tile. Here again, we have a unique conversion. %w(...) builds an Array of Strings from the "words" inside the parentheses. In this case, they're just individual letters and numbers. Those Arrays are indexed by *x* and *y*, and the results are concatenated with String addition (+).

The == method can quickly determine whether two Tile objects represent the same square by comparing both *x* and *y* values for each. If they both match, the objects are equal.

Finally, adjacent?() checks to see whether the passed Tile is near the current Tile. Both "adjacent" and "near" are tricky explanations, though; the method actually verifies that the Tiles are exactly a knight's jump from each other. Like the other methods of this class, the process is clever. First, dx and dy are filled with deltas for the two *x* and *y* values of each object. If both Tiles are valid?() and one delta is 1 while the other is 2, they are a knight's jump apart. The last line of this method uses an interesting combination of && and or operators. The difference in precedence allowed the author to avoid adding additional parentheses.

The next section of code puts those Tiles to work:

code/knights_travails/pretty.rb

```ruby
def knights_trip(start, finish, *forbidden)
  # First, build big bucket o' tiles.
  board = (0...64).collect { |n| Tile.new(n % 8, n / 8) }

  # Second, pull out forbidden tiles.
  board.reject! { |t| forbidden.include?(t) }

  # Third, prepare a hash, where layer 0 is just the start.
  # Remove start from the board.
  x = 0
  flood = { x => [start] }
  board.delete(start)

  # Fourth, perform a "flood fill" step, finding all board tiles
  # adjacent to the previous step.
  until flood[x].empty? or flood[x].include?(finish) do
    x += 1
    flood[x] = flood[x-1].inject([]) do |mem, obj|
      mem.concat(board.find_all { |t| t.adjacent?(obj) })
    end

    # Remove those found from the board.
    board.reject! { |t| flood[x].include?(t) }
  end

  # Finally, determine whether we found a way to the finish and, if so,
  # build a path.
  if not flood[x].empty?
    # We found a way. Time to build the path. This is built
    # backwards, so finish goes in first.
    path = [finish]

    # Since we got to finish in X steps, we know there must be
    # at least one adjacent to finish at X-1 steps, and so on.
    until x == 0
      x -= 1

      # Find in flood[x] a tile adjacent to the head of our
      # path. Doesn't matter which one. Make it the new head
      # of our path.
```

```
        jumps = flood[x].find_all { |t| t.adjacent?(path.first) }
        path[0,0] = jumps.sort_by { rand }.first
      end

      # Tada!
      path
    end
  end
```

The knights_trip() method does all the grunt work for this solution. You pass it the start, finish, and forbidden Tiles. It will return a path, if one can be found.

The method starts by building a Tile for every board square. After that, any forbidden Tiles are removed, so they won't be considered.

Next comes the heart of the algorithm. A Hash is created with pairs of search depth keys and value Arrays that represent all the Tiles at that depth. (Note that an Array could be used in place of the Hash, since the keys are ordered numerical indices.) The **until** loop fills in the Hash by searching each successive depth until running out of legal moves or locating the finish Tile. Each depth is built in the call to inject(), which just adds all the adjacent?() Tiles from the previous depth to an empty Array. Tiles are always removed from the board as they are added to the depth Hash to keep them from coming up as adjacent?() to later Tile searches. The final **if** statement builds the path by working backward through the depth search Hash one step at a time, looking for adjacent?() Tiles.

It takes only a little more code to finish the solution:

`code/knights_travails/pretty.rb`
```
# main
args = ARGV.collect { |arg| Tile.named(arg) }
if args.any? { |c| not c.valid? }
  puts "Invalid argument(s)!"
else
  trip = knights_trip(*args)
  if trip
    puts "Knight's trip: " + trip.join(", ")
  else
    puts "No route available!"
  end
end
```

This snippet puts the previous methods to use. ARGV is translated into Tile objects, and all those Tiles, if valid?(), are fed to knights_trip(). If a path is returned, it's printed. Otherwise, a route is not available, and a message relays this.

Or with Less Abstraction

For the sake of variety, here's my own solution to the problem:

`code/knights_travails/knights_travails.rb`

```ruby
#!/usr/local/bin/ruby -w

# chessboard in format {square => neighbors_array}
$board = Hash.new

# finds all the knight jumps from a given square
def neighbors( square )
  # consult cache, if it's available
  return $board[square] unless $board[square].nil?

  # otherwise calculate all jumps
  x, y = square[0] - ?a, square[1, 1].to_i - 1
  steps = Array.new

  [-1, 1].each do |s_off|
    [-2, 2].each do |l_off|
      [[s_off, l_off], [l_off, s_off]].each do |(x_off, y_off)|
        next_x, next_y = x + x_off, y + y_off

        next if next_x < 0 or next_x > 7
        next if next_y < 0 or next_y > 7

        steps << "#{(?a + next_x).chr}#{next_y + 1}"
      end
    end
  end

  # add this lookup to cache
  $board[square] = steps
end

# find a path using a breadth-first search
def pathfind( from, to, skips )
  paths = [[from]]
  until paths.empty? or paths.first.last == to
    path = paths.shift
    neighbors(path.last).each do |choice|
      next if path.include?(choice) or skips.include?(choice)
      paths.push(path.dup << choice)
    end
  end

  if paths.empty?
```

```
      nil
   else
     paths.shift.values_at(1..-1)
   end
end


# parse command-line arguments
if ARGV.size < 2 and ARGV.any? { |square| square !~ /^[a-h][1-8]$/ }
  puts "Usage:  #{File.basename(__FILE__)} START STOP [SKIPS]"
  exit
end
start, stop = ARGV.shift, ARGV.shift
skips       = ARGV


# find path and print results
p pathfind(start, stop, skips)
```

You can see that I begin by storing my chessboard in a global variable. I decided to use a Hash here, instead of the traditional Array. I store squares by name, with the value being an Array of knight jumps from that position, as shown in the neighbors() method.

In neighbors() the code calculates all possible knight jumps from the passed square. This is done by applying various combinations of -1, 1, -2, and 2 offsets while verifying that the squares stay inside the bounds of the board. Just before the method returns, the results are cached, so all future calls for the same square can just return the cached result.

The real work of this solution is done in pathfind(). This is a breadth-first search, expanding one jump each time through the loop until the target square is found or we run out of options. Notice that we skip the consideration of any square already in the path (to avoid doubling back) and forbidden squares provided by the user.

The last chunk of code is mainly just argument processing. We verify that ARGV holds at least two squares and that they are all valid, or we print a usage statement. The final line solves the problem and prints the results.

Additional Exercises

1. Alter your solution to "draw" the output. Print out an ASCII art version of the chessboard, with rank-and-file labels. Number each of the squares the knight will travel through in order. For example:

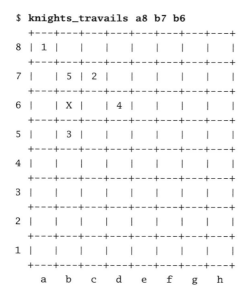

```
$ knights_travails a8 b7 b6
  +---+---+---+---+---+---+---+---+
8 | 1 |   |   |   |   |   |   |   |
  +---+---+---+---+---+---+---+---+
7 |   | 5 | 2 |   |   |   |   |   |
  +---+---+---+---+---+---+---+---+
6 |   | X |   | 4 |   |   |   |   |
  +---+---+---+---+---+---+---+---+
5 |   | 3 |   |   |   |   |   |   |
  +---+---+---+---+---+---+---+---+
4 |   |   |   |   |   |   |   |   |
  +---+---+---+---+---+---+---+---+
3 |   |   |   |   |   |   |   |   |
  +---+---+---+---+---+---+---+---+
2 |   |   |   |   |   |   |   |   |
  +---+---+---+---+---+---+---+---+
1 |   |   |   |   |   |   |   |   |
  +---+---+---+---+---+---+---+---+
    a   b   c   d   e   f   g   h
```

2. Expand your solution to take an integer as an optional final argument on the command line. When present, the solution should include exactly that many moves (without revisiting a square), or the program should report that it is not possible to make the trip in that many moves.

Answer **11**
From page 31

Sokoban

Implementing Sokoban is not hard. Here's a very brief solution from Dennis Ranke. Dennis decided to keep the levels in their text formats and lean on Ruby's text-processing strengths. This probably doesn't make for the prettiest of solutions, but it is short.

```ruby
code/sokoban/text_manip.rb
class Level
  def initialize(level)
    @level = level
  end

  def play
    while count_free_crates > 0
      printf "\n%s\n\n> ", self
      c = gets
      c.each_byte do |command|
        case command
          when ?w
            move(0, -1)
          when ?a
            move(-1, 0)
          when ?s
            move(0, 1)
          when ?d
            move(1, 0)
          when ?r
            return false
        end
      end
    end
    printf "\n%s\nCongratulations, on to the next level!\n", self
    return true
  end
```

```ruby
  private
    def move(dx, dy)
      x, y = find_player
      dest = self[x+dx, y+dy]
      case dest
        when ?#
          return
        when ?o, ?*
          dest2 = self[x+dx*2, y+dy*2]
          if dest2 == 32
            self[x+dx*2, y+dy*2] = ?o
          elsif dest2 == ?.
            self[x+dx*2, y+dy*2] = ?*
          else
            return
          end
          dest = (dest == ?o) ? 32 : ?.
      end
      self[x+dx, y+dy] = (dest == 32) ? ?@ : ?+
      self[x, y] = (self[x, y] == ?@) ? 32 : ?.
    end

    def count_free_crates
      @level.scan(/o/).size
    end

    def find_player
      pos = @level.index(/@|\+/)
      return pos % 19, pos / 19
    end

    def [](x, y)
      @level[x + y * 19]
    end

    def []=(x, y, v)
      @level[x + y * 19] = v
    end

    def to_s
      (0...16).map {|i| @level[i * 19, 19]}.join("\n")
    end
end

levels = File.readlines('sokoban_levels.txt')
levels = levels.map {|line| line.chomp.ljust(19)}.join("\n")
levels = levels.split(/\n {19}\n/).map{|level| level.gsub(/\n/, '')}

levels.each do |level|
  redo unless Level.new(level.ljust(19*16)).play
end
```

The play() method in the Level class is the primary interface for the code. It handles one level, start to finish, returning true if the level was solved and false if it was restarted. It checks for a level being solved by looping until count_free_crates() returns 0. That method uses scan() to count o characters. When a player enters a move command, work is handed off to the game-play routine move().

The first step to performing a move is to find the player. For that, find_player() uses a combination of index() and math[34] to locate an @ or + character. Once found, move() checks the square in front of the player. If it's a wall, it ignores the attempted move, and if it's open, the player moves. The special case is when there is a crate in front of the player. When found, move() looks behind the crate to ensure that the path is clear, and if it is, both crate and player are moved. All this testing and swapping is handled with the methods [] and [], which read and write tiles in the Level object.

The last chunk of Dennis's solution builds some Level objects and puts them to work. The external level file is parsed and cleaned up, storing each level in an Array. From there, it takes one call to each() to create a game.

Objectified Sokoban

Now let's examine a more abstract OO solution, sent in by Dave Burt:

```
code/sokoban/objectified.rb
module Sokoban

  NORTH = [-1,0]
  SOUTH = [1,0]
  EAST  = [0,1]
  WEST  = [0,-1]

  class SokobanError < StandardError
  end
end
```

Dave starts by setting up a Sokoban namespace and defining a few constants. He also creates a SokobanError for later exception handling.

Next, Dave starts defining classes to represent game world objects:

---

[34]This is a minor weakness of Dennis's solution. It works only for levels 19 characters wide and smaller. Standard Sokoban levels are 19 characters wide, but variations exist.

```
code/sokoban/objectified.rb
module Sokoban
  class Tile
    def self.create(chr = nil)
      case chr
      when '#' : Wall.new
      when ' ' : Floor.new
      when '@' : Floor.new(Person.new)
      when 'o' : Floor.new(Crate.new)
      when '.' : Storage.new
      when '+' : Storage.new(Person.new)
      when '*' : Storage.new(Crate.new)
      else       CharTile.new(chr)
      end
    end
    def to_s
      '~'
    end
  end

  class CharTile < Tile
    attr_reader :chr
    def initialize(chr)
      @chr = chr
    end
    def to_s
      chr
    end
  end

  class Wall < Tile
    def to_s
      '#'
    end
  end

  class Floor < Tile
    attr_accessor :resident
    def initialize(resident = nil)
      @resident = resident
    end
    def to_s
      return resident.to_s if resident
      ' '
    end
    def clear
      r = @resident
      @resident = nil
      r
    end
```

```
    def add(resident)
      throw SokobanError.new("Can't go there - this tile is full") if @resident
      @resident = resident
    end
    alias :<< :add
  end

  class Storage < Floor
    def has_crate?
      Crate === resident
    end
    def to_s
      case resident
      when Crate
        '*'
      when Person
        '+'
      else
        '.'
      end
    end
  end
end
```

Tile serves as a parent class for the different kinds of floor tiles, as well as a factory for creating the correct subclass from a character representation. CharTile is the basic concrete representation of nonessential board elements.

Wall is your most basic Tile type. It supports display with to_s(). It accomplishes its real goal as a barrier, simply by being a type other code can check against.

With Floor we're getting into basic game functionality. Floor objects can contain a single @resident, with the intended use being to hold Person or Crate objects. Notice that Floor's to_s() draws either itself or what is on it, as needed.

Storage inherits from Floor, adding a has_crate?() method that helps with level-complete checks. Note that Storage is careful to display itself and its contents in to_s().

The Person and Crate classes are simply types with a display method. They have no functionality other than to be passed around to different Tile objects. Here's a look at those:

```
code/sokoban/objectified.rb
module Sokoban
  class Crate
    def to_s
      'o'
    end
  end

  class Person
    def to_s
      '@'
    end
  end
end
```

Then we get to the meat of the program, which is the Level class:

```
code/sokoban/objectified.rb
module Sokoban
  class Level
    attr_reader :moves
    def initialize(str)
      @grid = str.split("\n").map{|ln| ln.split(//).map{|c| Tile.create(c) } }
      throw SokobanError.new('No player found on level') if !player_index
      throw SokobanError.new('No challenge!') if solved?
      @moves = 0
    end
    def [](r, c)
      @grid[r][c]
    end
    def to_s
      @grid.map{|row| row.join }.join("\n")
    end
    # returns a 2-element array with the row and column of the
    # player's position, respectively
    def player_index
      @grid.each_index do |row|
        @grid[row].each_index do |col|
          if @grid[row][col].respond_to?(:resident) &&
                          Person === @grid[row][col].resident
            return [row, col]
          end
        end
      end
      nil
    end
    def solved?
      # a level is solved when every Storage tile has a Crate
      @grid.flatten.all? {|tile| !(Storage === tile) || tile.has_crate? }
    end
    def move(dir)
      if [NORTH,SOUTH,EAST,WEST].include?(dir)
```

```
          pos = player_index
          target = @grid[pos[0] + dir[0]][pos[1] + dir[1]]
          if Floor === target
            if Crate === target.resident
              indirect_target = @grid[pos[0] + 2*dir[0]][pos[1] + 2*dir[1]]
              if Floor === indirect_target && !indirect_target.resident
                @grid[pos[0] + 2*dir[0]][pos[1] + 2*dir[1]] <<
                    @grid[pos[0] + dir[0]][pos[1] + dir[1]].clear
                @grid[pos[0] + dir[0]][pos[1] + dir[1]] <<
                    @grid[pos[0]][pos[1]].clear
                return @moves += 1
              end
            else
              @grid[pos[0] + dir[0]][pos[1] + dir[1]] <<
                  @grid[pos[0]][pos[1]].clear
              return @moves += 1
            end
          end
        end
        nil
      end
    end
end
```

Level objects build a @grid of Tile objects in initialize() to manage their state. The methods [] and to_s() provide indexing and display for the @grid. You can also easily locate the Person object in the @grid with player_index() and see whether the Level is complete with solved?().

The final method of Level is move(), which works roughly the same as Dennis's version. It finds the player and checks the square in the direction the player is trying to move. If a crate is found there, it also checks the square behind that one.

The rest of Dave's solution is an interactive user interface he provided for it:

`code/sokoban/objectified.rb`
```
module Sokoban
  # command-line interface
  def self.cli(levels_file = 'sokoban_levels.txt')
    cli_help = <<-end

      Dave's Cheap Ruby Sokoban  (c) Dave Burt 2004

      @ is you
      + is you standing on storage
      # is a wall
      . is empty storage
      o is a crate
```

```
                * is a crate on storage

        Move all the crates onto storage.

        to move:     n/k
                      |
                w/h -+- e/l
                      |
                     s/j
        to restart the level: r
        to quit: x or q or !
        to show this message: ?

        You can queue commands like this: nwwwnnnwnwwsw...

end

cli_help.gsub!(/\t+/,'  :  ')
puts cli_help

File.read(levels_file).split("\n\n").
                        each_with_index do |level_string, level_index|
  level = Level.new(level_string)
  while !level.solved? do
    puts level
    print 'L:' + (level_index+1).to_s + ' M:' + level.moves.to_s + ' > '
    gets.split(//).each do |c|
      case c
      when 'w', 'h'
        level.move(WEST)
      when 's', 'j'
        level.move(SOUTH)
      when 'n', 'k'
        level.move(NORTH)
      when 'e', 'l'
        level.move(EAST)
      when 'r'
        level = Level.new(level_string)
      when 'q', 'x', '!'
        puts 'Bye!'
        exit
      when 'd' # debug - ruby prompt
        print 'ruby> '
        begin
          puts eval(gets)
        rescue
          puts $!
        end
      when '?'
        puts cli_help
      when "\n", "\r", "\t", " "
```

```
        # ignore whitespace
      else
        puts "Invalid command: '#{c}'"
        puts cli_help
      end
    end
  end
  puts "\nCongratulations - you beat level #{level_index + 1}!\n\n"
      end
    end
end


if $0 == __FILE__
  Sokoban::cli
end
```

That's not as scary as it looks. The first half is a String of instructions printed to the user, and the second half is just a **case** statement that matches user input to all the methods we've been examining.

As you can see, this interface could be replaced with GUI method calls while still leveraging the underlying system. This wouldn't be any more work than building the command-line interface was.

Saving Your Fingers

This challenge touches on an interesting aspect of software design: interface. With a game, interface is critical. Dennis Ranke's and Dave Burt's games read line-oriented input, requiring you to push Enter (Return) to send a move. Although they do allow you to queue up a long line of moves, this tires my poor little fingers out, especially on involved levels.

That begs the question, why did they use this approach?

Portability would be my guess. Reading a single character from a terminal interface can get tricky, depending on which operating system you are running on. Here's how I do it on Unix:

```
def get_character
  state = `stty -g`
  begin
    system "stty raw -echo cbreak"
    @input.getc
  ensure
    system "stty #{state}"
  end
end
```

Here's one way you might try the same thing on Windows:

```
def read_char
  require "Win32API"

  Win32API.new("crtdll", "_getch", [], "L").Call
end
```

If you want your game to run on both, you may need to write code to detect the platform and use the proper method. Here's one way you might accomplish that:

```
begin
  require "Win32API"

  def read_char
    Win32API.new("crtdll", "_getch", [], "L").Call
  end
rescue LoadError
  def read_char
    state = `stty -g`

    begin
      system "stty raw -echo cbreak"
      @input.getc
    ensure
      system "stty #{state}"
    end
  end
end
```

That doesn't cover every platform, but I believe it will work with Windows and most Unix flavors (including Mac OS X). That may be enough for some purposes.

Another way to handle this would be to use the Curses library. Curses is standard Ruby but unfortunately is not so standard in the Windows world. A great advantage to this approach is being able to use the arrow keys, which makes for the best interface, I think.

Interface work can quickly get neck deep in external dependencies, it seems. Since games are largely defined by their interfaces, that makes for some complex choices. Maybe we should hope for a Swing-like addition to the Ruby Standard Library sometime in the future.

Additional Exercises

1. Modify your solution's interface so it responds immediately to individual keystrokes (without pressing Return).

2. Add a move counter, and modify your solution to track a lowest-moves score for each level.

3. Add a save-and-restore feature to your game to allow players to suspend play and resume the game at a later time.

4. Solve levels one through ten of Sokoban.

Answer **12**

From page 33

Crosswords

Let's break down a clean solution from Jim D. Freeze:

`code/crosswords/clean.rb`
```ruby
class CrossWordPuzzle
  CELL_WIDTH  = 6
  CELL_HEIGHT = 4

  attr_accessor :cell_width, :cell_height

  def initialize(file)
    @file        = file
    @cell_width  = CELL_WIDTH
    @cell_height = CELL_HEIGHT
    build_puzzle
  end

private
  def build_puzzle
    parse_grid_file
    drop_outer_filled_boxes
    create_numbered_grid
  end
end
```

Nothing tricky there. First, initialize some constants and variables. After that, the private method build_puzzle() outlines the process. Let's dig deeper into each of those steps. (In the code extracts that follow, parse_grid_file(), drop_outer_filled_boxes(), and create_numbered_grid() are all private methods of class CrossWordPuzzle.

`code/crosswords/clean.rb`
```ruby
def parse_grid_file
  @grid = File.read(@file).split(/\n/)
  @grid.collect! { |line| line.split }
  @grid_width  = @grid.first.size
  @grid_height = @grid.size
end
```

Step one: read the layout file, break it down by row at each \n character and by square at each space—this solution requires the spaces from the quiz description—and find the dimensions of the puzzle.

`code/crosswords/clean.rb`
```ruby
def drop_outer_filled_boxes
  loop {
    changed  = _drop_outer_filled_boxes(@grid)
    changed += _drop_outer_filled_boxes(t = @grid.transpose)
    @grid = t.transpose
    break if 0 == changed
  }
end

def _drop_outer_filled_boxes(ary)
  changed = 0
  ary.collect! { |row|
    r = row.join
    changed += 1 unless r.gsub!(/^X|X$/, ' ').nil?
    changed += 1 unless r.gsub!(/X | X/, '  ').nil?
    r.split(//)
  }
  changed
end
```

These two methods handle step two, dropping filled border squares. Jim uses a simple transpose() to perform a two-dimensional search and replace. More than one submission capitalized on this technique.

The search-and-replace logic is twofold: Turn all Xs at the beginning or end of the line into spaces, and turn all Xs next to spaces into spaces. Repeat this until there are no more changes. This causes the edges to creep in until all filled border squares have been eliminated.

Spring Cleaning

I removed a duplicate grid from create_numbered_grid() with a transpose-operate-transpose trick I learned earlier from drop_outer_filled_boxes in this same solution.

`code/crosswords/clean.rb`
```ruby
def create_numbered_grid
  mark_boxes(@grid)
  mark_boxes(t = @grid.transpose)
  @grid = t.transpose
  count = '0'
  @numbered_grid = []
  @grid.each_with_index { |row, i|
    r = []
    row.each_with_index { |col, j|
      r << case col
           when /#/ then count.succ!.dup
           else col
           end
    }
    @numbered_grid << r
  }
end
```

```ruby
# place '#' in boxes to be numbered
def mark_boxes(grid)
  grid.collect! { |row|
    r = row.join
    r.gsub!(/([X ])([\#_]{2,})/) { "#{$1}##{$2[1..-1]}" }
    r.gsub!(/^([\#_]{2,})/) { |m| m[0]=?#; m }
    r.split(//)
  }
end
```

Here's the third step, numbering squares. The approach here is much the same as step two. A combination of transpose() and gsub!() is used to mark squares at the beginning of words with a number sign. Words are defined as a run of number sign and/or underscore characters at the beginning of a line or after a filled box or open space. With number signs in place, it's a simple matter to replace them with an actual number.

Now that the grid has been doctored into the desired format, we need to wrap cells in borders and space and then stringify them. Here's the code for that. (Again, these are methods of CrossWordPuzzle.)

Spring Cleaning
I switched both calls to sprintf() in cell() to use the same format String. Both calls were using identical formatting but building it different ways. I thought using the same format String would make that easier to understand.

code/crosswords/clean.rb

```ruby
def cell(data)
  c = []
  case data
  when 'X'
    @cell_height.times { c << ['#'] * @cell_width }
  when ' '
    @cell_height.times { c << [' '] * @cell_width }
  when /\d/
    tb = ['#'] * @cell_width
    n  = sprintf("#%-#{@cell_width-2}s#", data).split(//)
    m  = sprintf("#%-#{@cell_width-2}s#", ' ').split(//)
    c << tb << n
    (@cell_height-3).times { c << m }
    c << tb
  when '_'
    tb = ['#'] * @cell_width
    m  = ['#'] + [' ']*(@cell_width-2) + ['#']
    c << tb
    (@cell_height-2).times { c << m }
    c << tb
  end
  c
end

def overlay(sub, mstr, x, y)
  sub.each_with_index { |row, i|
```

```
      row.each_with_index { |data, j|
        mstr[y+i][x+j] = data unless '#' == mstr[y+i][x+j]
      }
    }
  end

  def to_s
    puzzle_width  = (@cell_width-1)  * @grid_width  + 1
    puzzle_height = (@cell_height-1) * @grid_height + 1

    s = Array.new(puzzle_height) { Array.new(puzzle_width) << [] }

    @numbered_grid.each_with_index { |row, i|
      row.each_with_index { |data, j|
        overlay(cell(data), s, j*(@cell_width-1), i*(@cell_height-1))
      }
    }
    s.collect! { |row| row.join }.join("\n")
  end
```

The method to_s() drives the conversion process. It walks the doctored-up grid calling cell() to do the formatting and overlay() to place it in the puzzle.

cell() adds number sign borders and space as defined by the quiz, based on the cell type it is called on.

overlay() happily draws cells. However, it's called with placements close enough together to overlay the borders, reducing them to a single line. This "collapsing borders" technique is common in many aspects of programming. Examine the output of the mysql command-line tool, GNU Chess, or a hundred other tools. It's also common for GUI libraries to combine borders of neighboring elements.

With an Array of the entire puzzle assembled, to_s() finishes with few calls to join().

The "main" program combines the build and display:

`code/crosswords/clean.rb`
```
cwp = CrossWordPuzzle.new(ARGV.shift)
puts cwp.to_s
```

Passive Building

Now I want to examine another solution, by Trans Onoma. This one is a little trickier to figure out, but it uses a pretty clever algorithm. The following code slowly builds up the board, with only the knowledge it has at the time, constantly refining its image of the board until the entire puzzle is created. Here's the code:

```
code/crosswords/passive.rb
module CrossWord

  CELL_WIDTH = 6
  CELL_HEIGHT = 4

  def self.build( str )
    Board.new( str ).build
  end

  class Board
    def initialize( layout )
      b = layout.upcase  # upcase and duplicate input layout
      lines = b.split(/\n/)  # split into array of lines
      # split line into array of tokens...
      @board = lines.collect{ |line| line.scan(/[_X]/) }
      @cnt=0  # set cell counter (for numbering)
    end

    def height ; @height ||= @board.length ; end
    def width ; @width ||= @board[0].length ; end

    # the board builds itself as it is called upon
    def board(y,x)
      return nil if @board[y][x] == 'P' # pending resolution
      # resolution complete...
      return @board[y][x] if @board[y][x] != '_' and @board[y][x] != 'X'
      return @board[y][x] = 'u' if @board[y][x] == '_'
      # on edge...
      return @board[y][x] = 'e' if y==0 or x==0 or y==height-1 or x==width-1
      if @board[y][x] == 'X'  # could be edge or solid
        @board[y][x] = 'P' # mark as pending (prevents infinite recursion)
        return @board[y][x] = 'e' if  # edge if neighbor is edge
          board(y-1,x) == 'e' or board(y,x+1) == 'e' or
          board(y+1,x) == 'e' or board(y,x-1) == 'e'
      end
      return @board[y][x] = 's'  # else solid
    end

    # build the puzzle
    def build
      puzzle = Puzzle.new( height, width ) # new puzzle
      # edges must be done first since they clear spaces
      @board.each_with_index{ |line,y|
        line.each_index{ |x|
          type = board(y,x)
          puzzle.push(type,y,x,nil) if type == 'e'
        }
```

```ruby
      }
      # build-up all the solid and filled-in pieces
      @board.each_with_index{ |line,y|
        line.each_index{ |x|
          type = board(y,x)
          cnt = upper_left?(type,y,x) ? (@cnt += 1) : ''
          puzzle.push(type,y,x,cnt) if type != 'e'
      } }
      puzzle.to_s  # return the final product
    end


    # determines whether a cell should be numbered
    def upper_left?(type,y,x)
      return false if type != 'u'
      return true if y == 0 and board(y+1,x) == 'u'
      return true if x == 0 and board(y,x+1) == 'u'
      if x != width-1 and board(y,x+1) == 'u'
        return true if board(y,x-1) == 'e'
        return true if board(y,x-1) == 's'
      end
      if y != height-1 and board(y+1,x) == 'u'
        return true if board(y-1,x) == 'e'
        return true if board(y-1,x) == 's'
      end
      return false
    end

end

# Puzzle is a simple matrix
class Puzzle
  attr_reader :puzzle
  def initialize(height, width)
    @puzzle = ['']  # build a blank to work on
    (height*(CELL_HEIGHT-1)+1).times{ |y|
      (width*(CELL_WIDTH-1)+1).times{ |x| @puzzle.last << '.' }
      @puzzle << ''
    }
  end
  def push(type,y,x,cnt)
    c = space(type,cnt)
    ny = y * (CELL_HEIGHT - 1)
    nx = x * (CELL_WIDTH - 1)
    @puzzle[ny+0][nx,CELL_WIDTH] = c[0]
    @puzzle[ny+1][nx,CELL_WIDTH] = c[1]
    @puzzle[ny+2][nx,CELL_WIDTH] = c[2]
    @puzzle[ny+3][nx,CELL_WIDTH] = c[3]
  end
  def space(type,cnt)
    case type
    when "u"
```

```
        [ "#####",
          "#%-4s#" % cnt,
          "#    #",
          "#####" ]
      when "s"
        [ "#####" ] * 4
      when "e"
        [ "        " ] * 4
      end
    end
    def to_s ; @puzzle.join("\n") ; end
  end

end

if $0 == __FILE__
  $stdout << CrossWord.build( gets(nil) )
end
```

Since the beginning of the code just defines modules and classes that we don't yet know about, let's work backward. Start at the bottom with that standard **if** statement that generally signifies the "main" code.

We can see that the whole process is driven by a call to the module method CrossWord.build() (not to be confused with Board.build()). The method is passed the layout file slurped into a String and seems to return the entire result. Now we know where to look next!

Looking to that method, we can see that it doesn't do much. It constructs a Board object from the layout and calls build(). Jumping to Board.initialize(), we see that it too is pretty basic. It builds a two-dimensional Array of underscore and *X* characters, to match the layout file, with a call to scan(). It also starts a word counter. That leaves only build(), which is the primary workhorse of this code.

build() starts to get tricky, but it's basically three steps. First it creates a Puzzle, whatever that is. Then it does some strange dance with calls to board() and push(), primarily. Finally it returns a stringified Puzzle. Sounds like we need to get under the hood of that second class.

If Board is the programmatic representation of the layout, Puzzle represents the answer. Puzzle.initialize() just builds an Array of Strings the size of the square-expanded layout. All of these Strings are initialized to a run of periods.

Then we get to push(). That was one of those two methods that seemed to do a lot of the magic in build(). This method may not be ideally named, because it's really just a two-dimensional replace method. It calls space() and replaces a chunk of the puzzle's period characters with the actual square layout. If you look at space(), you'll see that it just returns one of the possible squares in a crossword based on the passed type.

Our knowledge has grown. Let's go back to build(). Now it should be easy to see that board() is returning the types that get sent on to push(). That's the last major method we need to decode.

board() just returns a type character, based on what the square actually is, at the location identified by the parameters. The method is a simple cascade, returning the first type it has proven. Note that it does recurse to check neighboring squares.

The final method called by build() is upper_left?(). It's another cascade method that locates the first square in a word so it can be numbered. When it returns true, build() increments its word counter and passes it on to push().

From there, Puzzle.to_s() gives us the final solution with a single call to join(). All of the periods will have been replaced by the actual squares at this point.

Those are two pretty different approaches, and there are certainly more. It's good to examine the thought process of others, because you never know when an idea will come in handy with your own future coding needs.

Additional Exercises

1. Modify your solution so it can take a scale as a command-line switch. A scale integer should be used as the width and height of output cells.

2. Enhance your program so that a list of clues can follow the board diagram in the input. Number and print these clues after the completed board, in two columns.

1-800-THE-QUIZ

Some problems are just easier to express with recursion. For me, this is one of those problems.

If you're not familiar with the idea, *recursion* is defining a method that calls itself. Sometimes we humans struggle to understand this concept of defining something in terms of itself, but it can make some programming challenges easier. Let's use this problem to explore the possibilities of recursion.

Word Signatures

The first step to solving this problem is doing the right work when you read in the dictionary. Come search time, we won't be interested in words at all, just groupings of digits. Each word in the dictionary can be encoded as the digits we would need to type on a phone. If we do that while we're reading them in and store them correctly, we can save ourselves much work down the road. First, let's begin a PhoneDictionary object and give it an encoding:

code/1_800_the_quiz/phone_words.rb
```ruby
require "enumerator"
class PhoneDictionary
  def self.encode( letter )
    case letter.downcase
    when "a", "b", "c"      then "2"
    when "d", "e", "f"      then "3"
    when "g", "h", "i"      then "4"
    when "j", "k", "l"      then "5"
    when "m", "n", "o"      then "6"
    when "p", "q", "r", "s" then "7"
    when "t", "u", "v"      then "8"
    when "w", "x", "y", "z" then "9"
    end
  end
end
```

> ### Beware of Recursion
>
> Though it simplifies some problems, recursion has its price. First, the repeated method calls can be slow. Depending on the size of the data you are crunching, you may feel the slowdown. Run the code in this chapter against different-sized dictionaries, and you'll start to see the penalty.
>
> Ruby also uses the C stack, which may not be set very deep by default, so it's best to avoid problems that need a lot of nested calls. The examples in this chapter are fine, because they never go deeper than eight levels. Make sure you stay aware of the limits in your own code.
>
> There's no such thing as recursive code that can't be unrolled to work as an iterative solution. If the restrictions bite you, you may just have to do the extra work.

My first instinct was to put the encoding into a constant, but I later decided a method would make it easy to replace (without a warning from Ruby). Not all phones are like mine, after all.

Obviously, you just give this method a letter, and it will give you back the digit for that letter.

Now, we need to set up our dictionary data structure. As with the rest of the methods in this quiz, this is an instance method in our PhoneDictionary class.

```
code/1_800_the_quiz/phone_words.rb
def initialize( word_file )
  @words = Hash.new { |dict, digits| dict[digits] = Array.new }
  ("0".."9").each { |n| @words[n] << n }
  %w{a i}.each { |word| @words[self.class.encode(word)] << word }

  warn "Loading dictionary..." if $DEBUG
  read_dictionary(word_file)
end
```

I use a Hash to hold word groups. A group is identified by the digit encoding (hash key) and is an Array of all words matching that encoding (hash value). I use Hash's default block parameter to create word group arrays as needed.

The next line is a trick to ease the searching process. Since it's possible for numbers to be left in, I decided to just turn individual numbers into words. This will allow bogus solutions with many consecutive numbers, but those are easily filtered out after the search.

Finally, I plan to filter out individual letter words, which many dictionaries include. Given that, I add the only single-letter words that make sense to me, careful to use encoding() to convert them correctly.[35]

At the bottom of that method, you can see the handoff to the dictionary parser:[36]

```
code/1_800_the_quiz/phone_words.rb
def read_dictionary( dictionary )
  File.foreach(dictionary) do |word|
    word.downcase!
    word.delete!("^a-z")

    next if word.empty? or word.size < 2 or word.size > 7

    chars  = word.enum_for(:each_byte)
    digits = chars.map { |c| self.class.encode(c.chr) }.join

    @words[digits] << word unless @words[digits].include?(word)
  end
end
```

This method is just a line-by-line read of the dictionary. I normalize the words to a common case[37] and toss out punctuation and whitespace. The method skips any words below two characters in length as well as any more than seven. Finally, words are split into characters, using the handy enum_for() from the Enumerator library (see the sidebar, on page 173, for details), and then digit encoded and added to the correct group. The code first verifies that a word wasn't already in the group, though, ensuring that our transformations don't double up any words.

The Search

With setup out of the way, we are ready to search a given phone number for word matches. First, we need a simple helper method that checks

---

[35]Be warned, this step assumes we are dealing with an American English dictionary.

[36]Notice the $DEBUG message hidden in this section of code. Ruby will automatically set that variable to true when passed the -d command-line switch, so it's a handy way to embed trace instructions you may want to see during debugging.

[37]Even though we're going to end up with uppercase results, I generally normalize case down, not up. Some languages make distinctions between concepts like title case and uppercase, so downcasing is more consistent.

a digit sequence against the beginning of a number. If it matches, we want it to return what's left of the original number:

```
code/1_800_the_quiz/phone_words.rb
def self.match( number, digits )
  if number[0, digits.length] == digits
    number[digits.length..-1]
  else
    nil
  end
end
```

With that, we are finally ready to search:

```
code/1_800_the_quiz/phone_words.rb
def search( number, chunks = Array.new )
  @words.inject(Array.new) do |all, (digits, words)|
    if remainder = self.class.match(number, digits)
      new_chunks = (chunks.dup << words)
      if remainder.empty?
        all.push(new_chunks)
      else
        all.push(*search(remainder, new_chunks))
      end
    else
      all
    end
  end
end
```

The idea here is to match numbers against the front of the phone number, passing the matched words and what's left of the String down recursively, until there is nothing left to match.

The method returns an Array of chunks, each of which is an Array of all the words that can be used at that point. For example, a small part of the search results for the quiz example shows that the number could start with the word *USER* followed by *-8-AX*, *TAX*, or other options:

```
[...
  [["user"], ["8"], ["aw", "ax", "ay", "by"]],
  [["user"], ["taw", "tax", "tay"]],
...]
```

The recursion keeps this method short and sweet, though you may need to work through the flow a few times to understand it.

The key to successful recursion is always having an *exit condition*, the point at which you stop recursing. Here, the method recurses only when there are remaining digits in the number. Once we've matched them all or failed to find any matches, we're done.

Enumerator: A Hidden Treasure

The Enumerator library is a hidden treasure of Ruby's standard library that was undocumented until very recently. Here's a quick tour to get you started using it today.

The main function of the library is to add an enum_for() method to Object, also aliased as to_enum(). Call this method, passing a method name and optionally some parameters, and you'll receive an Enumerable object using the passed method as each(). As you can see in the dictionary-parsing code of this chapter, that's a handy tool for switching Strings to iterate over characters, among other uses.

As an added bonus, the library adds two more iterators to Enumerable:

```
>> require "enumerator"
=> true
>> (1..10).each_slice(2) { |slice| p slice }
[1, 2]
[3, 4]
[5, 6]
[7, 8]
[9, 10]
=> nil
>> (1..10).each_cons(3) { |consecutive| p consecutive }
[1, 2, 3]
[2, 3, 4]
[3, 4, 5]
[4, 5, 6]
[5, 6, 7]
[6, 7, 8]
[7, 8, 9]
[8, 9, 10]
=> nil
```

Cleaning Up and Showing Results

Obviously the results returned from the search aren't printable as they stand. Let's use some more recursion to flatten the nested arrays down to strings.

code/1_800_the_quiz/phone_words.rb
```
def chunks_to_strings( chunks )
  chunk, *new_chunks = chunks.dup
  if new_chunks.empty?
    chunk.map { |word| word.upcase }
  else
    chunk.map do |word|
```

```
    chunks_to_strings(new_chunks).map { |words|  "#{word.upcase}-#{words}" }
  end.flatten
end
end
```

Again the idea behind this method is trivial: peel a single word group off, and combine it with all the other combinations generated through recursion of the remaining groups. Logically, the exit condition here is when we reach the final word group, and we can just return those words when that happens.

The class requires just one more public interface method to tie it all together:

code/1_800_the_quiz/phone_words.rb
```ruby
def number_to_words( phone_number )
  warn "Searching..." if $DEBUG
  results = search(phone_number)

  warn "Preparing output..." if $DEBUG
  results.map! { |chunks| chunks_to_strings(chunks) }
  results.flatten!
  results.reject! { |words| words =~ /\d-\d/ }
  results.sort!

  results
end
```

This method runs the workflow. Perform a search, convert the results to Strings, remove bogus results, clean up, and return the fruits of our labor. A caller of this method provides a phone number and receives ready-to-print word replacements.

Here's the last bit of code that implements the quiz interface:

code/1_800_the_quiz/phone_words.rb
```ruby
if __FILE__ == $0
  dictionary = if ARGV.first == "-d"
    ARGV.shift
    PhoneDictionary.new(ARGV.shift)
  else
    PhoneDictionary.new("/usr/share/dict/words")
  end

  ARGF.each_line do |phone_number|
    puts dictionary.number_to_words(phone_number.delete("^0-9"))
  end
end
```

Additional Exercises

1. Unroll the search() method presented in this chapter to build an iterative solution.

2. Benchmark the recursion and iterative versions of the code. What was the speed increase?

Texas Hold'em

There's a reason we spend a huge portion of our early computer science education just playing with sorting algorithms. Many programming challenges are completely or at least mostly solved by the proper sort. Poker hands are one of those problems.

Ruby's Sorting Tricks

A couple of sorting niceties in Ruby can make complex sorts a lot easier. Let's talk a little about those before we dig into the code that uses them.

First, if you're not familiar with sort_by(), now is a great time to fix that:

```
$ ruby -e 'p %w{aardvark bat catfish}.sort_by { |str| str.length }'
["bat", "catfish", "aardvark"]
```

With sort_by(), you can specify the criteria on which to sort the elements. You might specify the size of a String, for example. Behind the scenes, the elements are replaced with the result of the code block you passed, sorted, and then switched back to the original elements and returned.[38]

One other useful trick in Ruby is that Arrays themselves are sortable, and they order themselves by comparing each of their child elements in turn:

```
$ ruby -e 'p [[1, 5, 1], [1, 2, 3]].sort'
[[1, 2, 3], [1, 5, 1]]
```

You can even combine these two tricks for more sorting goodness. You can feed sort_by() an Array of criteria, which will be compared element by element to create an ordering of the original data. Let's look at some code that uses these tricks to deal with poker hands.

---

[38]sort_by() always returns a copy of the data. There is no sort_by!(), so just reassign if you want to replace the old values.

Sorting Cards

We're not trying to build a full poker game here, just a scoring system. Because of that, we don't need a very complex idea of cards. Even hands themselves can be just an Array of cards. Here's the setup:

```
code/texas_holdem/texas_hold_em.rb
require "enumerator"

Card = Struct.new(:face, :suit)

class Hand
  FACE_ORDER = %w{A K Q J T 9 8 7 6 5 4 3 2}
  HAND_ORDER = [ "Royal Flush", "Straight Flush", "Four of a Kind",
                 "Full House", "Flush", "Straight", "Three of a Kind",
                 "Two Pair", "Pair", "High Card" ]
  # the available orderings for cards in a hand
  ORDERS     = { :suit => lambda { |c, all| c.suit },
                 :high => lambda { |c, all| FACE_ORDER.index(c.face) },
                 :face_count => lambda do |c, all|
                   0 - all.find_all { |o| o.face == c.face }.size
                 end,
                 :suit_count => lambda do |c, all|
                   0 - all.find_all { |o| o.suit == c.suit }.size
                 end }

  def initialize( cards )
    @cards   = cards
    @name    = nil  # cache for hand lookup, so we only do it once
  end

  def order( *by )
    @cards = @cards.sort_by { |card| by.map { |e| ORDERS[e][card, @cards] } }
  end

  def hand
    return nil if @cards.size < 7
    @name ||= HAND_ORDER.find { |hand| send(hand.downcase.tr(" ", "_") + "?") }
  end
end
```

Here I pull in the Enumerator library for each_cons().[39] Then I prepare a simple Struct for Card objects, as promised. Hands are just an Array of Card objects.

You can see that I define some constants at the top of Hand for later use. The first two should be fairly obvious, but the third constant, ORDERS, is a little odd. It's easiest to figure out if you consider it with the order()

---

[39] See the sidebar, on page 173 if you're not familiar with the method.

method. This method is just a shell over sort_by() that feeds it an Array of criteria. You can use any criteria in the ORDERS Hash by Symbol name.

The last method in this section, hand(), just gives the name of the hand. It tries each possible hand, from best to worst, until it finds a match. This method has the desirable side effect of sorting the used cards to the front, since that's the system we used for matching hands.

Name the Hand

Now we need to look at each of the methods called by hand():

```
code/texas_holdem/texas_hold_em.rb
class Hand
  def royal_flush?
    order(:suit_count, :high) and cards =~ /^A(\w)K\1Q\1J\1T\1/
  end
end
```

Can't get much easier than that! Sorting by :suit_count, or the count of cards in a suit, and then by high card ensures that a royal flush will bubble right to the top of the stack. We haven't seen the cards() method yet, but it's easy to guess that it just stringifies the hand from what we see here. One Regexp later, we will know whether we found the royal family in a repeating suit.

The hardest hands to match in poker are the straights though:

```
code/texas_holdem/texas_hold_em.rb
class Hand
  def straight_flush?
    # it's not possible unless we have a Flush (also orders hand)
    return false unless flush?
    # save the full hand, so we can muck with it and restore it later
    saved_cards = @cards
    # trim hand to the Flush suit only
    @cards = @cards.reject { |card| card.suit != @cards[0].suit }
    # see if there is a Straight in the trimmed hand
    result = straight?
    # restore the hand, but preserve the order
    @cards = (@cards + saved_cards).uniq
    # return whether or not we found a Straight
    result
  end
end
```

This method checks for a flush, reduces the hand to just that suit, checks for a straight, and returns true only if it found both. The hand is also restored before returning.

To properly understand that, we need to see flush?() and straight?():

`code/texas_holdem/texas_hold_em.rb`

```ruby
class Hand
  def four_of_a_kind?
    order(:face_count, :high) and faces =~ /^(\w)\1\1\1/
  end

  def full_house?
    order(:face_count, :high) and faces =~ /^(\w)\1\1(\w)\2/
  end

  def flush?
    order(:suit_count, :high) and suits =~ /^(\w)\1\1\1\1/
  end

  def straight?
    # sort the cards by unique occurance, then value
    seen = Hash.new(0)
    @cards = @cards.sort_by do |card|
      [(seen[card.face] += 1), ORDERS[:high][card, @cards]]
    end
    # check for the special case, a low ace
    return true if faces =~ /^A5432/
    # walk through all possible Straights and check for match
    3.times do
      FACE_ORDER.each_cons(5) do |cards|
        return true if faces =~ /^#{cards.join}/
      end
      # rotate a card to the end and repeat checks two more times
      @cards << @cards.shift
    end
    # if we get this far, we didn't find one
    false
  end
end
```

Those first three methods, including flush?(), should be trivial by now. Again, we're just doing the lion's share of the work with fancy sorting.

The straight?() method is one of the exceptions where we have to do a bit more work. Sorting the cards by unique occurrence and then order will get us close but not all the way there. Note that we couldn't use the order() shortcut this time, because of the external Hash. Aces can be low or high in a straight, so we then have to check for the special case. From there we can check for each of the straights easy enough, but we have to do some extra card rotating since they may not be at the front of the hand.

The remaining hands are pure sort and match:

code/texas_holdem/texas_hold_em.rb

```ruby
class Hand
  def three_of_a_kind?
    order(:face_count, :high) and faces =~ /^(\w)\1\1/
  end

  def two_pair?
    order(:face_count, :high) and faces =~ /^(\w)\1(\w)\2/
  end

  def pair?
    order(:face_count, :high) and faces =~ /^(\w)\1/
  end

  def high_card?
    order(:high)
  end
end
```

We have only a few more methods in Hand:

code/texas_holdem/texas_hold_em.rb

```ruby
class Hand
  def to_s
    [hand, cards.scan(/../).join(" ")].reverse.join(" ").strip
  end

  def rating
    return nil if @cards.size < 7
    # rate hand, then each card in it for breaking ties
    [ 0 - HAND_ORDER.index(hand),
      @cards[0..4].map { |card| 0 - FACE_ORDER.index(card.face) } ]
  end

  private

  def cards() @cards.map { |card| "#{card.face}#{card.suit}" }.join end
  def faces() cards.scan(/(.).../).flatten.join                   end
  def suits() cards.scan(/.(.)/).flatten.join                     end
end
```

We can build up a String by finding the hand() and joining it with the cards(). We just have to be careful to find the hand() first, so the cards() will be in the proper order, which is why you see reverse() used in to_s().

The rating() method returns an Array, for use in sorting the hands to find a winner. A rating is first the rank of the type of hand and then the rank of the face of all five cards used in the hand. That handles breaking ties (a pair of kings beats a pair of tens) and "kickers" all in one Array.

Finally we have the **private** helpers used in all the hand matching.

Here's the tiny last bit of code to implement the quiz interface:

```
code/texas_holdem/texas_hold_em.rb
if __FILE__ == $0
  # read hands
  hands = ARGF.inject(Array.new) do |all, line|
    all << Hand.new(line.strip.split.map { |card| Card.new(*card.split("")) })
  end
  # rank hands, best to worst
  ratings = hands.map { |hand| hand.rating }.compact.sort { |a, b| b <=> a }
  # show results
  puts hands.map { |h| h.rating == ratings[0] ? "#{h} (Winner)" : h }
end
```

One last time, it's sorting to the rescue. We read the hands, order them by rating(), and then print them back out with an added (Winner) if they have the top rating. That even handles ties.

Additional Exercises

1. Expand your hand-naming output to include as much detail as possible. For example, "two pair—aces over kings."

2. Use as much of your solution code as possible to make a two player game of Texas hold'em. You can find complete rules of play at http://texasholdem.omnihosts.net/pokerrules.shtml.

Answer 15

From page 41

Solitaire Cipher

```
$ ruby solitaire.rb "CLEPK HHNIY CFPWH FDFEH"
YOURC IPHER ISWOR KINGX
$ ruby solitaire.rb "ABVAW LWZSY OORYK DUPVH"
WELCO METOR UBYQU IZXXX
```

That's what you should have seen, if you ran a working Solitaire cipher decryption script over the last two lines of the quiz.

There's nothing inherently difficult about this quiz. It's really just coding to a specification. Knowing that, our focus needs to be accuracy. A great way to achieve that is to use unit tests to validate the process. Another advantage to this approach is that the quiz itself already gave us a handful of test cases.

Testing a Cipher

The first part of the quiz describes encryption and decryption, so I started by yanking all the tests I could find out of the problem. That gave me a starting set of unit tests.

I will show all of my cipher tests together, but the truth is that I wrote them method by method. I would come up with some reasonable tests and then implement the code that makes them pass. Write more tests; write more code. What I'm describing is a popular software construction technique known as Test Driven Development (TDD).. This allowed me to work in very small steps that kept me from getting overwhelmed, and I recommend trying some projects this way, if you haven't already. It really can make it easier to iteratively work up to a complete solution.

OK, let's get to those tests:

`code/solitaire_cipher/tc_cipher.rb`

```ruby
#!/usr/local/bin/ruby -w

require "test/unit"
require "cipher"

class TestCipher < Test::Unit::TestCase
  def setup
    @keystream = Object.new
    class << @keystream
      def next_letter
        @letters.shift
      end

      def reset
        @letters = "DWJXH YRFDG TMSHP UURXJ".delete(" ").split("")
      end
    end
    @keystream.reset
    @cipher = Cipher.new(@keystream)
  end

  def test_normalize
    assert_equal( "CODEI NRUBY LIVEL ONGER",
                  Cipher.normalize("Code in Ruby, live longer!") )

    assert_equal( "YOURC IPHER ISWOR KINGX",
                  Cipher.normalize("Your cipher is working!") )
  end

  def test_text_to_chars
    assert_equal( [  3, 15,  4,  5,  9,
                    14, 18, 21,  2, 25,
                    12,  9, 22,  5, 12,
                    15, 14,  7,  5, 18 ],
                  Cipher.text_to_chars("CODEI NRUBY LIVEL ONGER") )

    assert_equal( [  4, 23, 10, 24,  8,
                    25, 18,  6,  4,  7,
                    20, 13, 19,  8, 16,
                    21, 21, 18, 24, 10 ],
                  Cipher.text_to_chars("DWJXH YRFDG TMSHP UURXJ") )
  end

  def test_chars_to_text
    assert_equal( "GLNCQ MJAFF FVOMB JIYCB",
                  Cipher.chars_to_text( [  7, 12, 14,  3, 17,
                                          13, 10,  1,  6,  6,
                                           6, 22, 15, 13,  2,
                                          10,  9, 25,  3,  2 ] ) )
  end
```

```ruby
  def test_encrypt
    assert_equal( "GLNCQ MJAFF FVOMB JIYCB",
                  @cipher.encrypt("Code in Ruby, live longer!") )
  end

  def test_decrypt
    assert_equal( "CODEI NRUBY LIVEL ONGER",
                  @cipher.decrypt("GLNCQ MJAFF FVOMB JIYCB") )

    @keystream.reset
    assert_equal( "YOURC IPHER ISWOR KINGX",
                  @cipher.decrypt("CLEPK HHNIY CFPWH FDFEH") )

    @keystream.reset
    assert_equal( "WELCO METOR UBYQU IZXXX",
                  @cipher.decrypt("ABVAW LWZSY OORYK DUPVH") )
  end
end
```

If you compare those with the quiz itself, you will see that I haven't really had to do any thinking yet. Those test cases were given to me for free.

How did I know the answers to the encrypted test cases before I had a working program? It's not just that I'm in close with the quiz creator, I assure you. I validated them with a deck of cards. There's no shame in a low-tech, by-hand dry run to make sure you understand the process you are about to teach to a computer.

The only decisions I have made so far are interface decisions. Running the cipher seems logically separate from keystream generation, so I decided that each would receive its own class and the latter could be passed to the constructor of the former. This makes it possible to build ciphers using a completely different method of keystream generation.

You can see that I mostly skip resolving what a keystream object will be at this point. I haven't come to that part yet, after all. Instead, I just build a generic object and use Ruby's singleton class syntax to add a couple of methods to it. Don't panic if you've never seen that syntax before; it's just a means to add a couple of methods to a single object.[40] The next_letter() method will be the only interface method Cipher cares about, and reset() is just a tool for testing.

Now we need to go from tests to implementation:

---

[40]For a more detailed explanation, see http://www.rubygarden.org/ruby?SingletonTutorial.

```ruby
class Cipher
  def self.chars_to_text( chars )
    chars.map { |char| (char + ?A - 1).chr }.join.scan(/.{5}/).join(" ")
  end

  def self.normalize( text )
    text =  text.upcase.delete("^A-Z")
    text += ("X" * (text.length % 5))
    text.scan(/.{5}/).join(" ")
  end

  def self.text_to_chars( text )
    text.delete("^A-Z").split("").map { |char| char[0] - ?A + 1 }
  end

  def initialize( keystream )
    @keystream = keystream
  end

  def decrypt( message )
    crypt(message, :-)
  end

  def encrypt( message )
    crypt(message, :+)
  end

  private

  def crypt( message, operator )
    c = self.class

    message  = c.text_to_chars(c.normalize(message))
    keystream = c.text_to_chars(message.map { @keystream.next_letter }.join)

    crypted = message.map do |char|
      ((char - 1).send(operator, keystream.shift) % 26) + 1
    end

    c.chars_to_text(crypted)
  end
end
```

Nothing too fancy appears in there, really. We have a few class methods that deal with normalizing the text and converting to and from text and IntegerArrays. The rest of the class uses these.

The two work methods are encrypt() and decrypt(), but you can see that they are just a shell over a single crypt() method. Encryption and decryption have only two minor differences. First, with decryption, the text is already normalized, so that step isn't needed. There's no harm in normalizing already normalized text, though, so I chose to ignore that difference completely. The other difference is that we're adding the letters in encryption and subtracting them with decryption. That was solved with a simple operator parameter to 3.

A Deck of Letters

With the Cipher object all figured out, I found myself in need of a keystream object representing the deck of cards.

Some solutions went pretty far down the abstraction path of decks, cards, and jokers, but that adds quite a bit of code for what is really a simple problem. Given that, I decided to keep the quiz's notion of cards as just numbers.

Once again, I took my testing straight from the quiz:

code/solitaire_cipher/tc_cipher_deck.rb

```ruby
#!/usr/local/bin/ruby -w

require "test/unit"

require "cipher_deck"

class TestCipherDeck < Test::Unit::TestCase
  def setup
    @deck = CipherDeck.new do |deck|
      loop do
        deck.move_down("A")
        2.times { deck.move_down("B") }
        deck.triple_cut
        deck.count_cut
        letter = deck.count_to_letter

        break letter if letter != :skip
      end
    end
  end

  def test_move_down
    @deck.move_down("A")
    assert_equal((1..52).to_a << "B" << "A", @deck.to_a)

    2.times { @deck.move_down("B") }
    assert_equal([1, "B", (2..52).to_a, "A"].flatten, @deck.to_a)
  end
```

```ruby
def test_triple_cut
  test_move_down

  @deck.triple_cut
  assert_equal(["B", (2..52).to_a, "A", 1].flatten, @deck.to_a)
end

def test_count_cut
  test_triple_cut

  @deck.count_cut
  assert_equal([(2..52).to_a, "A", "B", 1].flatten, @deck.to_a)
end

def test_count_to_letter
  test_count_cut

  assert_equal("D", @deck.count_to_letter)
end

def test_keystream_generation
  %w{D W J X H Y R F D G}.each do |letter|
    assert_equal(letter, @deck.next_letter)
  end
end
end
```

While writing these tests, I wanted to break them down into the individual steps, but those steps count on everything that has come before. That's why you see me rerunning previous steps in most of the tests. I had to get the deck back to the expected state.

You can see that I flesh out the next_letter() interface I decided on earlier more in these tests. The constructor will take a block that manipulates the deck and returns a letter. Then next_letter() can just call it as needed.

The idea with the previous design is that CipherDeck is easily modified to support other card ciphers. You can add any needed manipulation methods, since Ruby's classes are open, and then just pass in the block that handles the new cipher.

You can see from these tests that most of the methods simply manipulate an internal deck representation. The to_a() method will give you this representation in the form of an Array and was added just to make testing easy. When a method is expected to return a letter, a mapping is used to convert the numbers to letters.

Let's see how all of that comes out in code:

`code/solitaire_cipher/cipher_deck.rb`

```ruby
#!/usr/local/bin/ruby -w

require "yaml"

class CipherDeck
  DEFAULT_MAPPING = Hash[ *( (0..51).map { |n| [n +1, (?A + n % 26).chr] } +
                            ["A", :skip, "B", :skip] ).flatten ]

  def initialize( cards = nil, &keystream_generator )
    @cards = if cards and File.exists? cards
      File.open(cards) { |file| YAML.load(file) }
    else
      (1..52).to_a << "A" << "B"
    end
    @keystream_generator = keystream_generator
  end

  def count_cut( counter = :bottom )
    count = counter_to_count(counter)
    @cards = @cards.values_at(count..52, 0...count, 53)
  end

  def count_to_letter( counter = :top, mapping = DEFAULT_MAPPING )
    card = @cards[counter_to_count(counter)]
    mapping[card] or raise ArgumentError, "Card not found in mapping."
  end

  def move_down( card )
    if card == @cards.last
      @cards[1, 0] = @cards.pop
    else
      index = @cards.index(card)
      @cards[index], @cards[index + 1] = @cards[index + 1], @cards[index]
    end
  end

  def next_letter( &keystream_generator )
    if not keystream_generator.nil?
      keystream_generator[self]
    elsif not @keystream_generator.nil?
      @keystream_generator[self]
    else
      raise ArgumentError, "Keystream generation process not given."
    end
  end

  def save( filename )
    File.open(filename, "w") { |file| YAML.dump(@cards, file) }
  end
```

```ruby
def triple_cut( first_card = "A", second_card = "B" )
  first, second = @cards.index(first_card), @cards.index(second_card)
  top,   bottom = [first, second].sort
  @cards = @cards.values_at((bottom + 1)..53, top..bottom, 0...top)
end

def to_a
  @cards.inject(Array.new) do |arr, card|
    arr << if card.is_a? String then card.dup else card end
  end
end

private

def counter_to_count( counter )
  unless counter = {:top => :first, :bottom => :last}[counter]
    raise ArgumentError, "Counter must be :top or :bottom."
  end
  count = @cards.send(counter)
  if count.is_a? String then 53 else count end
end
end
```

Methods such as move_down() and triple_cut() are right out of the quiz and should be easy to understand. I've already explained next_letter() and to_a() as well.

The methods count_cut() and count_to_letter() are also from the quiz, but they have a strange counter parameter. You can pass either :top or :bottom to these methods, depending on whether you want to use the top card of the deck as your count or the bottom. You can see how these are resolved in the private method counter_to_count().

You can also see the mapping I mentioned in my description of the tests used in count_to_letter(). DEFAULT_MAPPING is straight from the quiz description, but you can override it for other ciphers.

The last point of interest in this section is the use of YAML in the constructor and the save() method. This allows the cards to be saved out in a YAML file, which can later be used to reconstruct a CipherDeck object. This is support for keying the deck, which I'll discuss a little more with the final solution.

A Test Suite and Solution

Following my test-then-develop strategy, I tied the test cases up into a trivial test suite:

> ## Joe Asks...
> ### How Secure is a Deck of Cards?
>
> Bruce Schneier set out to design Solitaire to be the first truly secure hand cipher. However, Paul Crowley has found a bias in the random number generation used by the cipher. In other words, it's not as strong as originally intended, and being a hand cipher, it does not compete with the more powerful forms of digital encryption, naturally.

`code/solitaire_cipher/ts_all.rb`

```ruby
#!/usr/local/bin/ruby -w

require "test/unit"

require "tc_cipher_deck"
require "tc_cipher"
```

Finally, I created a human interface in the format specified by the quiz:

`code/solitaire_cipher/solitaire.rb`

```ruby
#!/usr/local/bin/ruby -w

require "cipher_deck"
require "cipher"

card_file = if ARGV.first == "-f"
  ARGV.shift
  "cards.yaml"
else
  nil
end

keystream = CipherDeck.new(card_file) do |deck|
  loop do
    deck.move_down("A")
    2.times { deck.move_down("B") }
    deck.triple_cut
    deck.count_cut
    letter = deck.count_to_letter

    break letter if letter != :skip
  end
end
solitaire = Cipher.new(keystream)
```

```
if ARGV.size == 1 and ARGV.first =~ /^(?:[A-Z]{5} )*[A-Z]{5}$/
  puts solitaire.decrypt(ARGV.first)
elsif ARGV.size == 1
  puts solitaire.encrypt(ARGV.first)
else
  puts "Usage:  #{File.basename($PROGRAM_NAME)} MESSAGE"
  exit
end
```

```
keystream.save(card_file) unless card_file.nil?
```

The first and last chunks of code load from and save to a YAML file, if the -f command-line option is given. You can rearrange the cards in this file to represent the keyed deck, and then your cipher will keep it up with each run.

The second chunk of code creates the Solitaire cipher from our tools. This should be very familiar after seeing the tests.

Finally, the if block determines whether we're encrypting or decrypting as described in the quiz and calls the proper method, printing the returned results.

Additional Exercises

1. If you haven't already done so, cover your solution with some unit tests.

2. Refactor your solution so that the keystream generation is easily replaced, without affecting encryption or decryption.

3. Text the flexibility of your solution by implementing an alternate method of keystream generation, perhaps Mirdek.[41]

---

[41] http://www.ciphergoth.org/crypto/mirdek/description.html

English Numerals

The quiz mentioned brute force, so let's talk about that a bit. A naive first thought might be to fill an array with the numbers and sort. Does that work? No. Have a look:

```
$ ruby -e 'Array.new(10_000_000_000) { |i| i }'
-e:1:in 'initialize': bignum too big to convert into 'long' (RangeError)
	from -e:1:in 'new'
	from -e:1
```

Obviously, that code doesn't handle English conversion or sorting, but the point here is that Ruby croaked before we even got to that. An Array, it seems, is not allowed to be that big. We'll need to be a little smarter than that.

A second thought might be something like this:

```
code/english_numerals/brute_force.rb
first = num = 1
while num <= 10_000_000_000
  # English conversion goes here!
  first = [first, num].sort.first if num % 2 != 0
  num += 1
end
p first
```

That will find the answer. Of course, depending on your computer hardware, you may have to wait a couple of days for it. Yuck. We're going to need to move a little faster than that.

Grouping Numbers

The "trick" here is easy enough to grasp with a little more thought. Consider the numbers in the following list:

- ...
- Twenty-eight
- Twenty-nine
- Thirty
- Thirty-one
- Thirty-two
- Thirty-three
- ...

They are not yet sorted, but think of what will happen when they are. Obviously, all the twenties will sort together, and all the thirties will too, because of the leading word. Using that knowledge, we could check ten numbers at a time. However, when we start finding words like *thousand* or *million* at the beginning of our numbers, we can skip a lot more than ten. That's the secret to cracking this riddle in a reasonable time frame.

Coding an Idea

Now, let's look at some code that thinks like that from Eliah Hecht:

```
code/english_numerals/quiz.rb
class Integer

  DEGREE = [""] + %w[thousand million billion trillion quadrillion
  quintillion sextillion septillion octillion nonillion decillion
  undecillion duodecillion tredecillion quattuordecillion
  quindecillion sexdecillion septdecillion novemdecillion
  vigintillion unvigintillion duovigintillion trevigintillion
  quattuorvigintillion quinvigintillion sexvigintillion
  septvigintillion octovigintillion novemvigintillion trigintillion
  untregintillion duotrigintillion googol]

  def teen
    case self
    when 0: "ten"
    when 1: "eleven"
    when 2: "twelve"
    else    in_compound + "teen"
    end
  end

  def ten
    case self
    when 1: "ten"
    when 2: "twenty"
    else    in_compound + "ty"
    end
  end
end
```

```ruby
  def in_compound
    case self
    when 3: "thir"
    when 5: "fif"
    when 8: "eigh"
    else    to_en
    end
  end

  def to_en(ands=true)
    small_nums = [""] + %w[one two three four five six seven eight nine]
    if self < 10: small_nums[self]
    elsif self < 20: (self % 10).teen
    elsif self < 100:
      result = (self/10).ten
      result += "-" if (self % 10) != 0
      result += (self % 10).to_en
      return result
    elsif self < 1000
      if self%100 != 0 and ands
        (self/100).to_en(ands)+" hundred and "+(self%100).to_en(ands)
      else ((self/100).to_en(ands)+
        " hundred "+(self%100).to_en(ands)).chomp(" ")
      end
    else
      front,back = case (self.to_s.length) % 3
        when 0: [0..2,3..-1].map{|i| self.to_s[i]}.map{|i| i.to_i}
        when 2: [0..1,2..-1].map{|i| self.to_s[i]}.map{|i| i.to_i}
        when 1: [0..0,1..-1].map{|i| self.to_s[i]}.map{|i| i.to_i}
        end
      result = front.to_en(false) + " " + DEGREE[(self.to_s.length-1)/3]
      result += if back > 99: ", "
                elsif back > 0: ands ? " and " : " "
                else ""
                end
      result += back.to_en(ands)
      return result.chomp(" ")
    end
  end

end

medium_nums = (1..999).map{|i| i.to_en}
print "The alphabetically first number (1-999) is: "
puts first = medium_nums.min.dup
first_degree = Integer::DEGREE[1..-1].min
first << " " + first_degree
puts "The first non-empty degree word (10**3-10**100) is: "+first_degree
next_first = (["and"] + medium_nums).min
first << " " + next_first
```

```
puts "The next first word (numbers 1-999 + 'and' ) is: "+next_first
if next_first == "and"
  puts "Since the last word was 'and' , we need an odd number in 1..99."
  odd_nums = []
  (0..98).step(2){|i| odd_nums << medium_nums[i]}
  first_odd = odd_nums.min
  puts "The first one is: "+first_odd
  first << " " + first_odd
else # This will never happen; I can' t bring myself to write it.
end
puts "Our first odd number, then, is #{first}."
```

This code begins by adding methods to Integer to convert numbers to their English names. The teen(), ten(), and in_compound() methods are simple branches and easy to follow. The last method, to_en(), is the interesting code.

This method too is really just a big branch of logic. Note that the early ifs handle numbers less than ten, then teens, then numbers less that 100, and finally numbers less than 1000. Beyond that, the code switches strategies. You can see that the code splits the number into a front and a back. The front variable is set to the leading digits of the number, leaving the back holding all the digits that fit into three-digit groupings. The method then recurses to find words for both chunks, appending the proper DEGREE word to front and sprinkling with ands and commas as needed.

The final chunk of code is what actually solves the problem. It makes use of the programmer's logic to do very little work and solve a much bigger range than that presented in the quiz. Interestingly, it also explains how it is getting the answer. Here's a run:

```
The alphabetically first number (1-999) is: eight
The first non-empty degree word (10**3-10**100) is: billion
The next first word (numbers 1-999 + 'and' ) is: and
Since the last word was 'and' , we need an odd number in 1..99.
The first one is: eighty-five
Our first odd number, then, is eight billion and eighty-five.
```

Proper Grammar

If you're a grammar purist, the previous probably bothers you. Glenn P. Parker explained his frustration with his submitted solution:

> I'm afraid I could not bring myself to code up some random ill-defined method of expressing numbers in English, so I did it the way I was taught in school, using hyphens and absolutely no ands or commas. I think I've got Strunk & White on my side.

Removing the ands does change the answer, so let's examine Glenn's code:

code/english_numerals/grammatical.rb

```ruby
#!/usr/bin/ruby

class Integer

  Ones = %w[ zero one two three four five six seven eight nine ]
  Teen = %w[ ten eleven twelve thirteen fourteen fifteen
             sixteen seventeen eighteen nineteen ]
  Tens = %w[ zero ten twenty thirty forty fifty
             sixty seventy eighty ninety ]
  Mega = %w[ none thousand million billion ]

  def to_english
    places = to_s.split(//).collect {|s| s.to_i}.reverse
    name = []
    ((places.length + 2) / 3).times do |p|
      strings = Integer.trio(places[p * 3, 3])
      name.push(Mega[p]) if strings.length > 0 and p > 0
      name += strings
    end
    name.push(Ones[0]) unless name.length > 0
    name.reverse.join(" ")
  end

  private

  def Integer.trio(places)
    strings = []
    if places[1] == 1
      strings.push(Teen[places[0]])
    elsif places[1] and places[1] > 0
      strings.push(places[0] == 0 ? Tens[places[1]] :
                   "#{Tens[places[1]]}-#{Ones[places[0]]}")
    elsif places[0] > 0
      strings.push(Ones[places[0]])
    end
    if places[2] and places[2] > 0
      strings.push("hundred", Ones[places[2]])
    end
    strings
  end
end

# If there are command-line args, just print out English names.
if ARGV.length > 0
  ARGV.each {|arg| puts arg.to_i.to_english}
  exit 0
end
```

```ruby
# Return the name of the number in the specified range that is the
# lowest lexically.
def minimum_english(start, stop, incr)
  min_name = start.to_english
  start.step(stop, incr) do |i|
    name = i.to_english
    min_name = name if min_name > name
  end
  min_name
end

# Find the lowest phrase for each 3-digit cluster of place-values.
# The lowest overall string must be composed of elements from this list.
components =
  [ minimum_english(10**9, 10**10, 10**9),
    minimum_english(10**6, 10**9 - 1, 10**6),
    minimum_english(10**3, 10**6 - 1, 10**3),
    minimum_english(10**0, 10**3 - 1, 2) ]

$result = components[-1]
def search_combinations(list, selected = [])
  if elem = (list = list.dup).shift
    if list.empty?
      # Always include the final element from list in the selection.
      string = selected.dup.push(elem).join(" ")
      $result = string if $result > string
    else
      search_combinations(list, selected)
      search_combinations(list, selected.dup.push(elem))
    end
  end
  $result
end

puts search_combinations(components)
```

You can see that Glenn also extended the Integer class, in this case with a to_english() method. That method again works in digit trios. It breaks the number up into an Array of digits and then sends them to Integer.trio() in groups of three. Integer.trio() handles the small-number special cases and returns an Array of Strings, the English names. These are built up, until to_english() can join them to form the complete number.

Skipping the short command-line arguments test, the rest of the code is again the solution. The minimum_english() method is very similar to the brute-force code we were originally playing with, save that it uses an increment. Next, you can see the components Array is filled with the minimum_english() result for each three-digit group. (Note that the last group uses an increment of 2, to examine only odd numbers.)

While components actually holds the final answer in pieces now, a simple join() would be sufficient, Glenn avoids using his knowledge to skip steps. Instead, he defines search_combinations() to recursively join() each of the components, ensuring that the final union would sort first. The last line prints the result of that search: eight billion eight hundred eight million eight hundred eight thousand eight hundred eighty-five.

Additional Exercises

1. Write a program, using some of your code for this quiz if you like, that converts English numbers back into digit form.

2. The ability to convert numbers to and from English words comes in handy in many applications. Some people have used the code from this quiz in solutions to other quizzes. Convert your script so it still solves the quiz normally when run but just loads the converter methods when used in the **require** statement of another program.

3. Solve the quiz again, in the foreign language of your choice.

Answer 17
From page 49

Code Cleaning

Solving this quiz isn't really about the end result. It's more about the process involved. Here's a stroll through my process for the first script.

Timothy Byrd asked the right first question on Ruby Talk. To paraphrase, "What does this sucker do?" The programs used are semifamous, and if you follow Redhanded,[42] you probably already know.[43]

If you didn't, the -rcgi in the first line is a really big hint. -r is the command-line shortcut for a requiring library, in this case cgi. From there, it's pretty easy to assume that the script is a CGI script. That told me I needed to get it behind a web server to play with it.

Instant Web Serving

I could have put it behind Apache and worked with it that way, but I chose to use Ruby's standard WEBrick server instead. I'm glad I did too, because I ran into a few issues while getting it running that were super easy to see by watching WEBrick's responses in my terminal. Here's the WEBrick script I wrote to serve it up:

`code/code_cleaning/server.rb`
```ruby
#!/usr/bin/env ruby
require "webrick"

server = WEBrick::HTTPServer.new(:Port => 8080, :DocumentRoot => "cgi-bin")

['INT', 'TERM'].each do |signal|
  trap(signal) { server.shutdown }
end
server.start
```

---

[42] http://redhanded.hobix.com/

[43] http://redhanded.hobix.com/bits/batsmansFiveLineWiki.html

That's super basic WEBrick in action. Pull in the library, initialize a server with a port and document directory, set signal handlers for shutting down, and start it up. This server can handle HTML, ERB templates, and, most important here, CGI. Perfect.

I created the referenced cgi-bin directory right next to my server.rb script and dropped in a file with the code to test, named wiki.rb.

I then browsed over to http://localhost:8080/wiki.rb and was greeted by a Wiki HomePage. Now that I had it running, I felt like I could start dealing with the code and see what it was doing.

Finding the Hidden Wiki

The first thing I like to do with any code I can't read is to inject a lot of whitespace. It helps me identify the sections of code. A cool trick to get started with this in golfed/obfuscated Ruby code is a global find and replace of ; with \n. Then season with space, tab, and return to taste. Here's my spaced-out version:

```
code/code_cleaning/wiki_spaced.cgi
#!/usr/local/bin/ruby -rcgi

H, B = %w' HomePage w7.cgi?n=%s'

c = CGI.new 'html4'

n, d = c['n'] != '' ? c['n'] : H, c['d']

t = `cat #{n}`

d != '' && `echo #{t = CGI.escapeHTML(d)} > #{n}`

c.instance_eval {
  out {
    h1 { n } +
    a(B % H) { H } +
    pre { t.gsub(/([A-Z]\w+){2}/) { a(B % $&) { $& } } } +
    form("get") {
      textarea('d') { t } +
      hidden('n', n) +
      submit
    }
  }
}
```

Now we're getting somewhere. I can see what's happening. This silly little change opened my eyes to another problem immediately. Look at that second line:

```
H, B = %w' HomePage w7.cgi?n=%s'
```

I now know what the original script was called: w7.cgi. (The seventh
Wiki? Mauricio is an animal!) I modified the line to play nice with my
version:

```
H, B = %w' HomePage wiki.cgi?n=%s'
```

On to the next step. Let's clean up some of the language constructs
used here. We can spell out -rcgi, make those assignments slightly
more obvious, eliminate the ternary operator, clarify the use of the &&
operator, remove the dependency on the ugly $& variable, and swap
a few { ... } pairs with do ... end pairs. I thought about removing the
instance_eval() call, but to be honest I like that better than typing c. ten
times. Let's see how the code looks now:

`code/code_cleaning/wiki_lang.cgi`

```ruby
#!/usr/local/bin/ruby

require 'cgi'

H = 'HomePage'
B = 'wiki.cgi?n=%s'

c = CGI.new 'html4'

n = if c['n'] == '' then H else c['n'] end
d = c['d']

t = `cat #{n}`

`echo #{t = CGI.escapeHTML(d)} > #{n}` unless d == ''

c.instance_eval do
  out do
    h1 { n } +
    a(B % H) { H } +
    pre do
      t.gsub(/([A-Z]\w+){2}/) { |match| a(B % match) { match } }
    end +
    form("get") do
      textarea('d') { t } +
      hidden('n', n) +
      submit
    end
  end
end
```

The whole time I'm working on this code, I'm running it in my WEBrick
server, checking my changes, and learning more about how it func-

tions. One thing I'm noticing is an occasional usage statement from the cat command-line program:

```
cat: HomePage: No such file or directory
```

Sometimes it's being called on files that don't exist, probably before we add content to a given Wiki page. It still works (returning no content), but we can silence the warning. In fact, we should just remove the external dependency all together, making the code more portable in the process. In pure Ruby, `cat #{n}` is just File.read(n).

The other external dependency is on echo. We can fix that too—we open a File for writing and spit out the page contents. Here's where the code is now:

`code/code_cleaning/wiki_cat.cgi`

```ruby
#!/usr/local/bin/ruby

require 'cgi'

H = 'HomePage'
B = 'wiki.cgi?n=%s'

c = CGI.new 'html4'

n = if c['n'] == '' then H else c['n'] end
d = c['d']

t = File.read(n) rescue t = ''

unless d == ''
  t = CGI.escapeHTML(d)
  File.open(n, "w") { |f| f.write t }
end

c.instance_eval do
  out do
    h1 { n } +
    a(B % H) { H } +
    pre do
      t.gsub(/([A-Z]\w+){2}/) { |match| a(B % match) { match } }
    end +
    form("get") do
      textarea('d') { t } +
      hidden('n', n) +
      submit
    end
  end
end
```

At this point, I understand the code well enough to extend the variable names and add some comments, which should make its function pretty clear to others:

```
code/code_cleaning/wiki_clean.cgi
#!/usr/local/bin/ruby

# wiki.cgi

require 'cgi'

HOME = 'HomePage'
LINK = 'wiki.cgi?name=%s'

query = CGI.new 'html4'

# fetch query data
page_name    = if query['name'] == '' then HOME else query['name'] end
page_changes = query['changes']

# fetch file content for this page, unless it's a new page
content = File.read(page_name) rescue content = ''

# save page changes, if needed
unless page_changes == ''
  content = CGI.escapeHTML(page_changes)
  File.open(page_name, 'w') { |f| f.write content }
end

# output requested page
query.instance_eval do
  out do
    h1 { page_name } +
    a(LINK % HOME) { HOME } +
    pre do              # content area
      content.gsub(/([A-Z]\w+){2}/) do |match|
        a(LINK % match) { match }
      end
    end +
    form('get') do    # update from
      textarea('changes') { content } +
      hidden('name', page_name) +
      submit
    end
  end
end
```

That's probably as far as I would take that code, without trying to make any fundamental changes. The functionality is still pretty much the same (including limitations!), but it's much easier to follow how the code works.

The Other Program

I used pretty much the same process to decrypt Florian's code, so I won't bore you with a repeat. However, one additional tip that did help me through the complex renaming is worth mentioning here. When you need to rename a much-used method or variable, just do it, and then run the program. The error messages will give you the exact line numbers that need updating.

Here's the code I ended up with for Florian's program:

`code/code_cleaning/p2p_clean.rb`

```
#!/usr/local/bin/ruby
#
# p2p.rb
#
# Server: ruby p2p.rb password server public-uri private-uri merge-servers
# Sample: ruby p2p.rb foobar server druby://123.123.123.123:1337
#         druby://:1337 druby://foo.bar:1337
# Client: ruby p2p.rb password client server-uri download-pattern [list-only]
# Sample: ruby p2p.rb foobar client druby://localhost:1337 *.rb
###############################################################################
# You are not allowed to use this application for anything illegal
# unless you live inside a sane place. Insane places currently include
# California (see link) and might soon include the complete
# USA. People using this software are responsible for themselves. I
# can't prevent them from doing illegal stuff for obvious reasons. So
# have fun, and do whatever you can get away with for now.
#
# http://info.sen.ca.gov/pub/bill/sen/sb_0051-0100/-
#          sb_96_bill_20050114_introduced.html
###############################################################################

require 'drb'

# define utility methods
def create_drb_object( uri )
  DRbObject.new(nil, uri)
end

def encode( uri )
  [PASSWORD, uri].hash
end

def make_safe( path )
  File.basename(path[/[^|]+/])
end

# parse command-line options
PASSWORD, MODE, URI, VAR, *OPTIONS = ARGV
```

```ruby
class Server                          # define server operation
  new.methods.map{ |method| private(method) unless method[/_[_t]/] }

  def initialize
    @servers = OPTIONS.dup
    add(URI)
    @servers.each do |u|
      create_drb_object(u).add(URI) unless u == URI
    end
  end

  attr_reader :servers

  def add( z = OPTIONS )
    @servers.push(*z).uniq!
    @servers
  end

  def list( code, pattern )
    if encode(URI) == code
      Dir[make_safe(pattern)]
    else
      @servers
    end
  end

  def read( file )
    open(make_safe(file),  "rb").read
  end
end

if MODE["s"]     # server
  DRb.start_service(VAR, Server.new)
  sleep
else             # client
  servers = create_drb_object(URI).servers
  servers.each do |server|
    files = create_drb_object(server).list(encode(server), VAR).map do |f|
      make_safe f
    end
    files.each do |file|
      if OPTIONS[0]
        p(file)
      else
        open(file,  "wb") do |f|
          f << create_drb_object(server).read(file)
        end
      end
    end
  end
end
```

Additional Exercises

1. Find another obfuscated program but in another language you are familiar with. Translate it to clean Ruby code.

2. Create a golfed Ruby program for use as an email signature. The program should be four lines or fewer and have no more than 80 characters per line.

Banned Words

The general idea behind a lot of solutions to this quiz is pretty basic: try a big list (probably the whole list in this problem), and if that gets blocked, divide it into smaller lists and try again. This approach is known as *divide and conquer*.

When one of these chunks of words gets through, we know that every word in that chunk is clean. The higher up in our search that happens, the more work that saves us. Because of that, this solution is ideal when there aren't a lot of banned words, as would probably be the case in the real-world example of this quiz.

Here's my own solution as the most basic example of this process:

`code/banned_words/basic.rb`

```ruby
#!/usr/bin/env ruby

require "filter"

### my algorithm ###
def isolate( list, test )
  if test.clean? list.join(" ")
    Array.new
  elsif list.size == 1
    list
  else
    left, right = list[0...(list.size / 2)], list[(list.size / 2)..-1]
    isolate(left, test) + isolate(right, test)
  end
end

### test code ###
# choose some random words to ban
words = ARGF.read.split " "
filter = LanguageFilter.new words.select { rand <= 0.01 }

# solve
```

```
start = Time.now
banned = isolate words, filter
time = Time.now - start

# display results
puts "#{words.size} words, #{banned.size} banned words found"
puts "Correct?  #{filter.verify banned}"
puts "Time taken: #{time} seconds"
puts "Calls: #{filter.clean_calls}"
puts "Words:"
puts banned.map { |word|  "\t" + word }
```

isolate() is a recursive routine that takes an Array of words and a test
filter and returns the banned words. If the entire word list passes a
clean?() test, we return an empty Array (no banned words in the given
list). If we don't get an OK from clean?() and we have only one word in
the list, we've found a banned word and we return the one-word Array
itself to show that. Finally, if we didn't pass clean?() and we have more
than one word, we divide the list in half, call isolate() on each half, and
combine the results of both of those calls. Eventually, this drills down
to find all the banned words.

Of course, those are just the basics.

Dividing the word list in half at each step may not be the optimal
approach, especially when there are many banned words. Some solutions played around with different ratios and tried to find a fast way
to eliminate many words. Cutting the word list in thirds at each step
seemed to work well, as did using 10% of the word list size. These both
have the advantage of not needing any more external knowledge.

Defining Word Boundaries

The LanguageFilter class from the quiz is far from perfect. It
doesn't gracefully handle things such as apostrophes and plu-
rals. Even some languages trip it up. Defining a "word" is not
a very simple task. The code was left dumbed down to make
it easy to follow and use but may need to be modified to work
with your dictionary.

Doing Even Fewer Checks

Wayne Vucenic found a very clever optimization. If we check a big list and it gets banned, and then we split it up and check the first half and it comes back clean, we know the second half would be banned and can skip the check. That could save a significant number of messages that we would otherwise need to send. Let's examine that code:

`code/banned_words/optimized.rb`

```ruby
require "test_harness"

class YourAlgorithm < RQ9Algorithm
  # Returns an array containing all banned words from @words
  def run()
    if @words.empty?
      []
    else
      find_banned(@words)
    end
  end

  # Returns an array containing all banned words from words
  # words.size is > 0
  def find_banned(words)
    if words.size == 1
      @filter.clean?(words[0]) ? [] : words
    elsif @filter.clean?(words.join(' '))
      []
    else
      split_index = words.size / 2
      if @filter.clean?(words[0...split_index].join(' '))
        # There is at least one banned word in 0..-1, but not in
        # 0...split_index, so there must be one in split_index..-1
        find_banned_there_is_one(words[split_index..-1])
      else
        # From the test above we know there is a banned word in 0...split_index
        find_banned_there_is_one( words[0...split_index]) +
                          find_banned(words[split_index..-1] )
      end
    end
  end

  # Returns an array containing all banned words from words
  # words.size is > 0
  # Our caller has determined there is at least one banned word in words
  def find_banned_there_is_one(words)
    if words.size == 1
      # Since we know there is at least one banned word and since there is
      # only one word in the array, we know this word is banned without
      # having to call clean?
      words
```

```
        else
          split_index = words.size / 2
          if @filter.clean?(words[0...split_index].join(' '))
            # There is at least one banned word in 0..-1, but not in 0...split_index
            # so there must be one in split_index..-1
            find_banned_there_is_one(words[split_index..-1])
          else
            # From the previous test we know there is a banned word
            # in 0...split_index
            find_banned_there_is_one( words[0...split_index]) +
                                find_banned(words[split_index..-1] )
          end
        end
      end
    end
end
```

This code is designed to work with a test harness, written by Jannis Harder.[44] All you really need to know is that when run() is called, @words holds an Array of words in the dictionary, and @filter holds the language filter from the quiz.

The exciting work happens in find_banned(). It works similarly to the first example we looked at, except for that final **if** clause. When it's determined that there must be one banned word in the bunch, work gets handed off to find_banned_there_is_one(), which is smart enough to skip some checks, as I described previously. It doesn't always get to bypass the second check, but it's often enough to save a significant number of calls. Wayne's code found the answers with the least amount of checks on most of the examples in the test harness.

Additional Exercises

1. Try to improve LanguageFilter's notion of what a word is as discussed in the sidebar, on page 210.

2. If you used a divide-and-conquer approach, try to isolate the best number of chunks to divide the list into at each step, without any outside knowledge of the word list.

---

[44]You can find the test harness files at banned_words/test_harness.rb and banned_words/test.rb.

Secret Santas

The Secret Santas quiz is one of those problems that seems trivial at first glance but turns out to be trickier than expected. Some solutions seem to work but have subtle problems. Let's examine a naive solution.

When I first encountered this problem, I tried the following process:

1. Collect a list of players from the input.
2. Duplicate that list into a list of Santas, and shuffle.
3. For each player, filter the Santa list to remove anyone with an identical family name, and choose the first Santa from the filtered list.
4. Remove the chosen Santa from the list of Santas.
5. Print the current Santa-to-player match.
6. Repeat until all names are assigned.

That translates to Ruby easily enough:

code/secret_santa/naive.rb
```
players = ARGF.read.split("\n")
santas  = players.sort_by { rand }

while players.size > 0
  santa = santas.select { |s| s[/ \w+$/] != players[0][/ \w+$/] }.first
  santas.delete(santa)

  puts "#{santa} -> #{players.shift}"
end
```

All we need are some names, and we can test that solution. The test data from the quiz was picked to show off how tricky this problem can get. However, it might take several runs to see a problem. We can make the test even trickier by considering three families, one member each:

```
code/secret_santa/trickydata
Mr. Gray
Mr. Thomas
Mr. Matsumoto
```

Let's try a couple of tests:

```
james> ruby naive.rb < trickydata
Mr. Matsumoto -> Mr. Gray
Mr. Gray -> Mr. Thomas
Mr. Thomas -> Mr. Matsumoto
james> ruby naive.rb < trickydata
Mr. Thomas -> Mr. Gray
Mr. Gray -> Mr. Thomas
 -> Mr. Matsumoto
```

The first run goes just as expected, but what happened to the second run? Let's break it down:

1. Mr. Thomas was assigned as a Santa for Mr. Gray.
2. Mr. Gray was then assigned as the Santa for Mr. Thomas.
3. Then we're stuck! There are no matches left for Mr. Matsumoto. The only Santa left is Mr. Matsumoto himself, and we're filtering him out of the choices.

Depending on how you implement the previous steps, you should see incorrect output, as we did with my example, or get stuck in an infinite loop trying to find a matching Santa. Now that we know this problem has teeth, let's look at other options.

Notifying Santas

Obviously, printing out the list won't work if the person running the Santa selection script wants to play. When this quiz was originally posted to Ruby Talk, it required sending emails to the Santas to notify them who they would be giving gifts to. This is how I handle the game my friends play each year.

I've simplified the problem for the sake of this book, but luckily Ruby makes email sending trivial with Net::SMTP, in the standard library.

Using a Random Sort

One way to get a working mix of Santas to players is to use a random sort. The idea of a random sort is very basic: generate random matchups until we find a correct mix.

One way to code that up is as follows:

`code/secret_santa/random.rb`
```ruby
def correct_match?( givers, receivers )
  receivers.each_with_index do |who, i|
    return false if who[/ \w+$/] == givers[i][/ \w+$/]
  end
  return true
end

players = ARGF.read.split("\n")

begin
  santas = players.sort_by { rand }
end until correct_match?(santas, players)

santas.each_with_index do |s, i|
  puts "#{players[i]} -> #{s}"
end
```

This solution just shuffles *santas* until correct_match?() verifies that none of the matchups share family names. That ensures no one will have themselves or a common family member, of course.

This method does give us a good random shuffle of the matchups, but unfortunately, the performance is far from stellar. Depending on the number of players, how the families break down, and a little bit of bad luck, this program can take considerable time to run.

If you just need to assign Santas for a small group of friends something like the previous code may be adequate. However, if you're running a Secret Santa game for your company and you have a good number of employees, you may need to dig a little deeper for a solution.

A Ring of Players

Another way to approach this problem is to use a circular list. With this technique, you place all the players in a circle. While arranging players, or with an extra pass of processing afterward, you need to separate family members so they are not directly next to each other. From there, assigning Santas is as easy as matching everyone to the player next to them in the circle, as shown in Figure 1.3, on the following page.

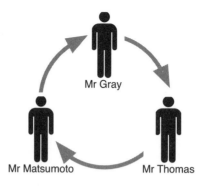

Mr Gray

Mr Matsumoto   Mr Thomas

Figure 1.3: Assigning from a Circular List

Algorithms like this are far more efficient than a random sort. However, this type of assignment is not truly random and does not allow for all possible permutations. Consider this: in a circular list approach, it is impossible for two players to be assigned to each other as Santas. That's not to say this is unacceptable. Some groups may even prefer this behavior. If you like the random feel, though, you'll need a different approach.

Grouping

Another common strategy for solving this problem is to divide all the players into groups by family. Then Santas are selected for players not in the same grouping.

This strategy is trickier than it sounds. It's common to see errors similar to naive.rb, infinite loops, or matchups that don't cover all possible permutations with this approach.

However, Niklas Vermont Frykholm submitted an error-free solution using family grouping that does produce random matches:

code/secret_santa/grouping.rb
```ruby
class Array
  def random_member(&block)
    return select(&block).random_member if block
    return self[rand(size)]
  end
  def count(&block)
    return select(&block).size
  end
end
```

```ruby
class Person
  attr_reader :first, :family
  def initialize(first, family)
    @first, @family = first, family
  end
  def to_s() "#{first} #{family}" end
end

class AssignSanta
  def initialize(persons)
    @persons = persons.dup
    @santas = persons.dup
    @families = persons.collect {|p| p.family}.uniq
    @families.each do |f|
      if santa_surplus(f) < 0
        raise "No santa configuration possible"
      end
    end
  end

  # Key function - extra santas available for a family
  #    if this is negative - no santa configuration is possible
  #    if this is 0 - next santa must be assigned to this family
  def santa_surplus(family)
    return @santas.count {|s| s.family != family} -
           @persons.count {|p| p.family == family}
  end

  def call
    while @persons.size() > 0
      family = @families.detect do |f|
        santa_surplus(f)==0 and
          @persons.count{|p| p.family == f} > 0
      end
      person = @persons.random_member do |p|
        family == nil || p.family == family
      end
      santa = @santas.random_member do |s|
        s.family != person.family
      end
      yield(person, santa)
      @persons.delete(person)
      @santas.delete(santa)
    end
  end
end

people = STDIN.read.split("\n").map do |line|
  first, family = line.chomp.split(' ', 2)
  Person.new(first, family)
end
```

```
assigner = AssignSanta.new(people)
assigner.call do |person, santa|
  puts "#{person} -> #{santa}"
end
```

The call() method does most of the work. call() selects players and then random Santas, from different family groups, to complete matchups. However, although it works, it constantly avoids painting itself into a corner with the use of the utility method santa_surplus().

santa_surplus() tracks the number of Santas still available for each family group. The program uses this to avoid leaving itself no valid matches in future iterations. As any other selection is allowed, this solution provides a random mix, eventually touching on all possible permutations.[45]

Climbing a Hill

A final type of solution is generally known as a "hill climbing" algorithm. Dennis Ranke explains his version nicely:

> I start by assigning a random Santa to everyone without caring about the constraints. Then I go through the list of people, and for each one not having a correct Santa, I swap Santas with someone else so that both have correct Santas afterward. As far as I can see, this will fail only when no solution is possible and should be reasonably unbiased.

Put another way, you start with a random (and likely quite incorrect) match-up and then correct it one swap at a time. Hill climbing is an efficient solution in many programming challenges.

Here's the code to match the description:

`code/secret_santa/hillclimb.rb`
```
class Person
  attr_reader :first, :last
  attr_accessor :santa

  def initialize(line)
    m = /(\S+)\s+(\S+)/.match(line)
    raise unless m
    @first = m[1].capitalize
    @last = m[2].capitalize
```

---

[45]Niklas posted his own mathematical analysis of his code to Ruby Talk. You can read that message at http://ruby-talk.org/cgi-bin/scat.rb/ruby/ruby-talk/114760.

```
      end

    def can_be_santa_of?(other)
      @last != other.last
    end
  end

  input = STDIN.read

  people = []
  input.each_line do |line|
    line.strip!
    people << Person.new(line) unless line.empty?
  end

  santas = people.dup
  people.each do |person|
    person.santa = santas.delete_at(rand(santas.size))
  end

  people.each do |person|
    unless person.santa.can_be_santa_of? person
      candidates = people.select { |p|
        p.santa.can_be_santa_of?(person) && person.santa.can_be_santa_of?(p)
      }
      raise if candidates.empty?
      other = candidates[rand(candidates.size)]
      temp = person.santa
      person.santa = other.santa
      other.santa = temp
    end
  end

  people.each do |person|
    printf "%s %s -> %s %s\n", person.santa.first, person.santa.last,
           person.first, person.last
  end
```

Santas are randomly assigned in the first people.each iteration and then swapped until correct in the following people.each iteration. Notice that candidates is filtered to include only valid matches, so each swap is assured to take us closer to a correct mix. If there are no candidates at any point, we cannot step closer to a correct solution, and thus we know that a match is impossible with this input.

Additional Exercises

1. Prove that your solution is or is not truly random. You can do this by writing another script that runs your solution repeatedly,

looking for all the possible permutations.

2. Add email support to your solution so that all players just see a message containing the person they are to play Santa for.

3. It's not uncommon for people to forget their person and ask to see the name again. Have your program save a copy of the match list, and provide an interface for resending the selection email to a given player.

Barrel of Monkeys

Let's jump right into a solution and explore aspects of this problem as we go along. Here's a helper class from my own code:

code/barrel_of_monkeys/barrel_of_monkeys.rb

```ruby
class Song
  def initialize( title, artist, duration )
    @title    = title
    @artist   = artist
    @duration = duration.to_i / 1000
  end

  attr_reader :title, :artist, :duration

  def starts_with(  )
    @title[/[A-Za-z0-9]/].downcase
  end

  def ends_with(  )
    @title[/[A-Za-z0-9](?=[^A-Za-z0-9]*$)/].downcase
  end

  def ==( other )
    @title == other.title and @artist == other.artist
  end

  def to_s(  )
    "#{@title} (by #{@artist} - #{@duration} seconds)"
  end
end
```

This class wraps song data. Aside from the accessors, an equality test, and a String conversion method, I define methods for getting the first and last characters of the song title. These methods use Regexps to find a letter or numeral in the proper place.

That leads us to questions about how to handle the names. I took the easy way out, along with most other submitters, which boils down to the fact that I don't try to clean up the names. There are lot of issues with those names, as there would be with any random sample, and you would need a lot of very careful rules to produce good results from them.

Quiz creator Gavin Kistner made a heroic attempt to fix the names with good results. Gavin's best trick was to convert numerals to English words so they could be matched normally. Unfortunately, the truth is that a human eye could probably normalize any list of names in about the time it took Gavin to build the code that works for some lists. I think that's just one of those areas where the computer isn't much help.

Let's move on to my playlist-building code:

```
code/barrel_of_monkeys/barrel_of_monkeys.rb
def build_playlist( start, finish, songs )
  playlists = [[start]]

  until playlists.empty? or
        playlists.first.last.ends_with == finish.starts_with
    playlist = playlists.shift
    next unless songs.include? playlist.last.ends_with

    songs[playlist.last.ends_with].each do |song|
      next if playlist.find { |s| song.ends_with == s.ends_with }
      playlists << (playlist.dup << song)
    end
  end

  if playlist.empty?
    nil
  else
    playlists.shift << finish
  end
end
```

Building a playlist is really a path-finding problem in disguise, and my method is just a simple breadth-first search. We don't need to search all the way to the end song, though; we can stop as soon as we have a song that ends with the letter the last song begins with. Otherwise, it's vanilla searching.

The parameters to this method are the start and finish songs for the playlist and the songs database. It worth noting that songs is expected to be a Hash of SongArrays, with the keys being the common letter a group of Song titles begin with. This makes for faster searching.

The process is as follows: First, make a list of paths initialized with a single path that contains only the starting point. Then, enter a loop that ends when the list of paths is empty or the first path in the list contains the endpoint. In that loop, pull the first path off the list, expand that path into a list of paths that all take one step further to the final point of the path, and add all those paths to the end of the paths list.

The only trick in doing this kind of a search is to be careful not to double back on your self, which is usually done by making sure a path doesn't already contain the point you're about to add. I modified that here to make sure no song already in the list ends with the same letter as the one we are about to add.

Then the final chunk of the method just returns the results with the last song added. This is always the shortest playlist, in terms of the number of songs it contains.

Here's the set-up interface code:

```
code/barrel_of_monkeys/barrel_of_monkeys.rb
unless ARGV.size == 2
  puts "Usage: #{File.basename($0)} START_SONG END_SONG"
  exit
end

warn "Reading song list..."
if File.exist? "song_list.cache"
  songs = File.open("song_list.cache", "r") { |file| Marshal.load(file) }
else
  require "rexml/document"

  songs = Hash.new

  xml = File.open("SongLibrary.xml", "r") { |file| REXML::Document.new(file) }
  xml.elements.each("Library/Artist") do |artist|
    artist.elements.each("Song") do |song|
      name = song.attributes["name"]
      next unless name =~ /[A-Za-z0-9]/

      new_song = Song.new( name, artist.attributes["name"],
                           song.attributes["duration"] )
      songs[new_song.starts_with] ||= Array.new
      songs[new_song.starts_with] << new_song
    end
  end

  File.open("song_list.cache", "w") { |file| Marshal.dump(songs, file) }
end
warn "Song list complete."
```

```
start_name, finish_name = ARGV.map { |name| name.downcase }
start = nil
songs.values.each do |song_list|
  start = song_list.find { |song| song.title.downcase.index(start_name) }
  break if start
end
finish = nil
songs.values.each do |song_list|
  finish = song_list.find { |song| song.title.downcase.index(finish_name) }
  break if finish
end
if start.nil?
  puts "Couldn't find #{start_name} in song list."
  exit
end
if finish.nil?
  puts "Couldn't find #{finish_name} in song list."
  exit
end
puts
puts "Start song:  #{start}"
puts "  End song:  #{finish}"
puts
```

After I check for usage with the two song names I'm expecting, the main problem to deal with is reading the song library. You can examine the **else** clause for my read strategy, which is REXML 101. This proved to be quite slow (around four seconds). When I got to testing my code, that became annoying very fast. I decided to speed it up by marshaling a cache file that loads in less than a second.[46] I just write the file after the first REXML load and then check and favor it in the future (the **if** clause).

A lot of submitters used similar strategies. One person used YAML instead of Marshal, but the result was the same if not quite as fast. Another solution is to parse the XML yourself with Regexps, which is fast and not too tricky with the provided file but obviously isn't as robust as using REXML.

The other issue to look at in the song-loading code is how they are stored internally. I wanted to make the lookups as fast as possible when I'm building playlists, which meant not combing through an entire Array to find songs. Instead, I stored them in a Hash by the let-

---

[46]I originally had a default Proc set for the Hash, but I had to remove it to get the Hash past Marshal.

ter they start with. Each letter is a key matched with an Array of Song objects whose names begin with that letter.

Finally, the set-up code locates the songs for which the user requested a playlist. You can easily see that my Hash structure doesn't bend well to this, since I have to use each() and find() to locate them. However, I need to do it only these two times at the beginning, so I thought it was an acceptable trade.

There's just a tiny little bit of code left to run the actual search process:

```
code/barrel_of_monkeys/barrel_of_monkeys.rb
warn "Building playlist..."
playlist = build_playlist(start, finish, songs)
warn "Playlist complete."

puts
if playlist.nil?
  puts "A playlist could not be found, between the selected songs."
else
  puts playlist
end
```

That's as simple as it looks. Find the playlist, and display it. We'll know whether no match is possible because the build_playlist() returns nil when it runs out of paths to try.

Fancy Searching

My solution doesn't handle durations or any other options. For that, let's walk through an option-driven solution by Dave Burt:

```
code/barrel_of_monkeys/barrel_with_options.rb
#
# A Song has a name, an artist, a duration, and an optional id
#
class Song
  def initialize(name, artist, duration = nil, id = 0)
    @name = name
    @artist = artist
    @duration = duration
    @id = id
  end
  attr_accessor :name, :artist, :duration, :id
  def basic_name
    @name.gsub(/\s*([\[(]).*\1\s*$/, '').gsub(/\bfeat.*$/, '')
  end
  def to_s
    "#@artist - #@name (#{@duration.min_sec})"
  end
```

```ruby
    def inspect
      to_s
    end


    # and, for the barrels of monkeys:

    def first_letter
      m = basic_name.match(/([a-z])/i)
      m[1].downcase if m
    end
    def last_letter
      m = basic_name.match(/([a-z])[^a-z]*$/i)
      m[1].downcase if m
    end
  end
```

This data class is very close to my version that we've already examined. The basic_name() method does minimal attempts to clean up the songs names, but again this is nothing complete.

code/barrel_of_monkeys/barrel_with_options.rb

```ruby
class Integer
  #
  # Display a time in milliseconds as m:ss
  #
  def min_sec
    "#{self/60000}:%02d" % (self/1000 % 60)
  end


  #
  # Display a time in milliseconds as h:mm:ss
  #
  def hr_min_sec
    "#{self/3600000}:%02d:%02d" % [self/60000 % 60, self/1000 % 60]
  end
end


class Array
  #
  # Return the sum of the durations of the elements
  #
  def total_duration
    inject(0) {|memo, song| memo + song.duration }
  end


  #
  # Return a string listing the contents of this array as a playlist, with
  # an appropriate header
  #
  def playlist_string
    i = 0
```

```
      "<Playlist tracks: #{size}, duration: #{total_duration.hr_min_sec}>\n" +
      map {|song| " #{i += 1}. #{song}\n" }.join
    end
end
```

Next we have a handful of helper methods added to Integer and Array. These methods cover Song playlist output. Additionally, total_duration() is a tool for adding up all the durations in an Array of Song objects.

Now let's get to the option-filled search code:

`code/barrel_of_monkeys/barrel_with_options.rb`

```
#
# A barrel of monkeys seems to be a set of songs with the capability to
# return playlists whose successive songs match last to first letter.
#
class BarrelOfMonkeys
  def initialize(songs)
    @songs = songs
  end
  attr_accessor :songs

  #
  # Index songs by first letter
  #
  def build_index
    @songs_by_first_letter = {}
    @songs.each do |song|
      (@songs_by_first_letter[song.first_letter] ||= []) << song \
        if song.first_letter
    end
    self
  end

  #
  # Searches @songs for barrel of monkeys playlists that match the given
  # criteria. The first letter in the title of each successive song in
  # each playlist is always the same as the last letter in the prior song.
  #
  # These are the allowed criteria (all are optional):
  #   first_letter     Playlists' first songs must begin with this letter
  #   last_letter      Playlists' last songs must end with this letter
  #   min_songs        Playlists must have at least this many songs
  #   max_songs        Playlists may have no more than this many songs
  #   target_songs     Only return playlists with as close as possible to
  #                    this number of songs
  #   min_duration     Playlists must run at least this many milliseconds
  #   max_duration     Playlists must run for no more milliseconds than this
  #   target_duration  Only return playlists with as close as possible to
  #                    this duration in milliseconds
  #   exclude_songs    Playlists must not include any songs included here
```

```ruby
#
def playlists(criteria = {})
  first_letter = criteria[:first_letter].downcase rescue nil
  last_letter = criteria[:last_letter].downcase rescue nil
  min_songs = criteria[:min_songs] || 1
  max_songs = criteria[:max_songs] || 1.0 / 0.0
  target_songs = criteria[:target_songs]
  min_duration = criteria[:min_duration] || 0
  max_duration = criteria[:max_duration] || 1.0 / 0.0
  target_duration = criteria[:target_duration]
  exclude_songs = criteria[:exclude_songs] || []

  build_index unless @songs_by_first_letter

  # build list of songs starting with required first letter
  result = (@songs_by_first_letter[first_letter] || @songs).map do |song|
    [song] unless exclude_songs.include? song
  end.
  delete_if {|song| song.nil? }

  # to each of those, add playlists starting with their last letter
  # (recursively, depth-first(!))
  if max_songs > 1
    result.map do |playlist|
      playlist_duration = playlist.total_duration
      playlists(
        :first_letter => playlist[-1].last_letter,
        :last_letter => last_letter,
        :min_songs => [min_songs - 1, 0].max,
        :max_songs => max_songs - 1,
        :target_songs => target_songs && target_songs - 1,
        :min_duration => min_duration - playlist_duration,
        :max_duration => max_duration - playlist_duration,
        :target_duration => target_duration &&
                            target_duration - playlist_duration,
        :exclude_songs => exclude_songs | playlist
      ).map do |subplaylist|
        playlist + subplaylist if subplaylist
      end
    end.each do |playlist|
      result.concat(playlist.to_a)
    end
  end

  # remove all playlists with the wrong last letter
  if last_letter
    result.delete_if {|pl| pl.last.last_letter != last_letter }
  end

  # remove all playlists with too few songs or too short or too long a
  # duration
```

```ruby
    result.delete_if do |pl|
      pl.size < min_songs or
      not pl.total_duration.between?(min_duration, max_duration)
    end

    # if a specific duration was requested, find the closest
    if target_duration
      closest_duration = result.inject(1.0/0.0) do |memo, pl|
        [ memo, (pl.total_duration - target_duration).abs ].min
      end
      result.delete_if do |pl|
        (pl.total_duration - target_duration).abs != closest_duration
      end
    end

    # if a specific number of songs were requested, find the closest
    if target_songs
      closest_songs = result.inject(1.0/0.0) do |memo, pl|
        [ memo, (pl.size - target_songs).abs ].min
      end
      result.delete_if do |playlist|
        (playlist.size - target_songs).abs != closest_songs
      end
    end

    result
  end
end
```

The hundred-pound gorilla in here is clearly BarrelOfMonkeys.playlists(). Luckily, the comments walk you through it pretty well. I'll just add some additional remarks to that.

You should notice that this is a recursive depth-first search. Because it does walk all the way down the very large song list and then basically back up until it finds what it's looking for, search times can get mighty hefty. Profiling and tuning may be able to clear up some of this, but the truth is that it's probably not the most efficient search format for large playlists.

On a more positive note, you can see the impressive set of options supported here. These are mostly handled at the tail end of the method where playlists are pruned if they don't match the desired criteria. Many clever ideas are hiding in here, so be sure and glance at how all this works.

```
code/barrel_of_monkeys/barrel_with_options.rb
if $0 == __FILE__

  print "Loading..."

  # HighLine::Dave
  # http://www.dave.burt.id.au/ruby/highline/dave.rb
  require 'highline/dave'
  require 'yaml'
  SONG_LIST = YAML.load_file("SongLibrary.yaml")

  barrel_of_monkeys = BarrelOfMonkeys.new(SONG_LIST)
  barrel_of_monkeys.build_index

  puts "done."

  begin

    t = Time.now

    criteria = {
      :first_letter => ask(
        "What letter should the first song start with?", /^[a-z]$/i),
      :last_letter => ask(
        "What letter should the last song end with?", /^[a-z]$/i),
      :min_songs => ask(
        "Minimum songs in playlist:", 1),
      :max_songs => ask(
        "Maximum songs in playlist (more than 3 could take a while):",
        SONG_LIST.size),
      :target_songs => ask(
        "Target number of songs: [no target]",
        Integer, :default => false, :display_default => false),
      :min_duration => ask(
        "Minimum duration in milliseconds:", 0),
      :max_duration => ask(
        "Maximum duration in milliseconds:", Integer, 1.0/0.0),
      :target_duration => ask(
        "Target duration in milliseconds: [no target]",
        Integer, :default => false, :display_default => false),
    }
    print "Generating playlists..."

    playlists = barrel_of_monkeys.playlists(criteria)

    puts "done in #{Time.now - t} seconds."
    puts "Found #{playlists.size} playlist#{'s' unless playlists.size == 1}:"
    puts playlists.map{|pl| pl.playlist_string }

  end while ask("Another barrel of monkeys?", FalseClass)
end
```

Finally, we have the code that loads a YAML version of the song list, asks the user an impressive set of configuration questions using Dave's HighLine library, runs the search, and reports results.

Additional Exercises

1. Modify your code to support as many of Dave's criteria as possible.

2. Spend some time profiling your search and looking for ways to speed it up. My own code is a bit sluggish with the example "Que Sera" to "Zaar." Can you beat my time on that tricky search, a little more than five seconds on my box?

Amazing Mazes

Let's look into Dominik Bathon's code. It is a nice algorithm and lightning quick! On my machine, it makes and solves mazes faster than the other solutions can make them. Even better, it uses a complex internal representation (mainly for speed) yet still comes out with clean algorithms. I was quite impressed by that.

Let's get to the code. Dominik starts off by defining a helper method in Hash:

```
code/amazing_mazes/fast_maze.rb
class Hash

  # find the key with the smallest value, delete it and return it

  def delete_min_value
    return nil if empty?
    minkey=min=nil
    each { |k, v|
      min, minkey=v, k if !min || v<min
    }
    delete(minkey)
    minkey
  end
end
```

The comment pretty much explains what's going on there. Each pair in the Hash is compared by value. The pair with the lowest value is deleted, and the key for that value is returned.

The Internal Bits

On to the interesting parts. Here's the start of the main class used by the solution:

```
code/amazing_mazes/fast_maze.rb
# Maze represents the maze ;-)
#
# Cells/positions in the maze are represented by Numbers (from 0 to
# w*h-1), each position corresponds to x/y coordinates, you can
# convert between positions and coordinates by coord2pos and
# pos2coord.
#
# The walls for each position are stored in the String @data. The
# walls for position p are stored in the first two bits of @data[p],
# and the other bits are unused. If 1 one is set, then p has a north
# wall; if bit 2 is set, then p has a west wall.
#
# Maze#generate generates a (random) maze using the method described
# at http://www.mazeworks.com/mazegen/mazetut/
#
# Maze#shortest_path uses Dijkstra's shortest path algorithm, so it
# can not only find shortest paths in perfect mazes, but also in mazes
# where different paths between two positions exist.

class Maze
  attr_reader :w, :h # width, height

  def initialize(w, h)
    @w, @h=[w, 1].max, [h, 1].max
    @wh=@w*@h
    @neighbors_cache={}
    set_all_walls
  end
end
```

I know this code is mostly comments, but you'll want to read it. It's interesting information, and it introduces you to the internal format the code uses.

After the comment, we see some readers defined and some simple initialization work. Set a width and height, ensuring they are both at least 1. Nice use of max() there. Calculate width times height or the total number of cells, initialize a cache, and call set_all_walls().

That means we need some more code:

```
code/amazing_mazes/fast_maze.rb
class Maze
  def set_all_walls
    # set all bits
    @data=3.chr * (@wh)
    nil
  end
```

```ruby
  def clear_all_walls
    # all except outer border
    @data=0.chr * (@wh)
    # set north walls of row 0
    w.times { |i| @data[i] |= 1 }
    # set west walls of col 0
    h.times { |i| @data[i*w] |= 2 }
    nil
  end
end
```

OK, now we start to get tricky. Remember the initial comment about using bits for the walls. We're tracking only two walls here, north and west. Of course, cells can still have up to four walls, but your east wall is just your neighbor's west wall, and your south wall is the north wall of the cell below you.

What do you get if you turn two bits on? *3.* The set_all_walls() method translates that to a character and duplicates it for every cell. The result is a string representing the entire maze with all the walls turned on.

That should make clear_all_walls() more obvious. This time we want no walls so we don't set any bits. Translate *0* to a character, and duplicate. However, we still need the edges of the maze. All cells in the top row need a north wall (set the *1* bit). Then all the cells in the first column need a west wall (set the *2* bit). That makes up the rest of the method.

Ready for the next chunk?

`code/amazing_mazes/fast_maze.rb`
```ruby
class Maze
  # positions in path will be printed as "X"
  def to_s(path=[])
    ph={}
    path.each { |i| ph[i]=true }
    res=""
    h.times { |y|
      w.times { |x|
        res << "+" << ((@data[y*w+x] & 1 > 0) ? "--" : "   ")
      }
      res << "+\n"
      w.times { |x|
        res << ((@data[y*w+x] & 2 > 0) ? "|" : " ")
        res << (ph[y*w+x] ? " X " : "   ")
      }
      res << "|\n"
    }
    res << ("+--"*w) << "+"
  end
```

```
    def inspect
      "#<#{self.class.name} #{w}x#{h}>"
    end
  end
```

The to_s() method draws mazes. The first two lines fill a Hash with the solution path, if one is given. The Hash is indexed in the same way as the maze String, and values can be **true** (if it's on the path) or the default **nil** (when it's not).

The rest of that method does the drawing. It walks row by row with h.times down the maze drawing cells. The first w.times call handles the north walls. First it adds a plus, and then it adds a horizontal line if the *1* bit is set or spaces if it's not. Next we need another plus and a newline. Now the second w.times block handles the west wall and path. First it checks to see whether the *2* bit is set for the current cell, outputting a vertical line if it is and a space if it's not. Then the path is checked. If this cell is on the path, it's filled with an *X*, and if it's not, the code adds a space.

The last two lines of the method are important. They ensure a final vertical line is always added to the end of a row and a final horizontal line is placed at the end of each column of the maze. This handles the east and south borders of the maze, which are not covered by the bits.

The other method, inspect(), returns a class name, width, and height.

`code/amazing_mazes/fast_maze.rb`
```
class Maze
  # maze positions are cell indices from 0 to w*h-1
  # the following functions do conversions to and from coordinates
  def coord2pos(x, y)
    (y % h) * w + (x % w)
  end
  def pos2coord(p)
    [p % w, (p / w) % h]
  end
end
```

These converters were explained in the initial comment, and they are explained again here. No surprises here.

`code/amazing_mazes/fast_maze.rb`
```
class Maze
  # returns valid neighbors to p, doesn't care about walls
  def neighbors(p)
    if ce=@neighbors_cache[p]; return ce; end
    res=[p-w, p+w]
    res << p-1 if p%w > 0
```

```
      res << p+1 if p%w < w-1
      @neighbors_cache[p] = res.find_all { |t| t>=0 && t<@wh }
    end
end
```

This returns indices of the up to four neighboring cells. It caches this lookup the first time it does it, since it will never change. The first line uses the cache if it has already been figured. The second line adds the cell above and the cell below. Note that these numbers are found by simple math and could be outside the bounds of the maze. The next two lines add the left and right cells. We're more careful with our math here, because a wrong answer could look right: the last cell of the first row is "left" of the first cell of the second row in our one-dimensional String that holds the maze data. The final line stores the indices to the cache and returns them, after using find_all() to eliminate any bogus numbers that crept in.

`code/amazing_mazes/fast_maze.rb`
```ruby
class Maze
  def wall_between?(p1, p2)
    p1, p2=[p1, p2].sort
    if p2-p1==w # check north wall of p2
      @data[p2] & 1 > 0
    elsif p2-p1==1 # check west wall of p2
      @data[p2] & 2 > 0
    else
      false
    end
  end
  def set_wall(p1, p2)
    p1, p2=[p1, p2].sort
    if p2-p1==w # set north wall of p2
      @data[p2] |= 1
    elsif p2-p1==1 # set west wall of p2
      @data[p2] |= 2
    end
    nil
  end
  def unset_wall(p1, p2)
    p1, p2=[p1, p2].sort
    if p2-p1==w # unset north wall of p2
      @data[p2] &= ~1
    elsif p2-p1==1 # unset west wall of p2
      @data[p2] &= ~2
    end
    nil
  end
end
```

These three methods are all very similar. Given two cells, the first checks whether there is a wall between them, the second sets the wall between them, and the third unsets it. The *ifs* figure out whether we are talking about a north wall or a west wall. The rest is bit testing or setting.

Making a Maze

On to maze generation:

```
code/amazing_mazes/fast_maze.rb
class Maze
  # generate a (random) perfect maze
  def generate(random=true)
    set_all_walls
    # (random) depth first search method
    visited={0 => true}
    stack=[0]
    until stack.empty?
      n=neighbors(stack.last).reject { |p| visited[p] }
      if n.empty?
        stack.pop
      else
        # choose one unvisited neighbor
        np=n[random ? rand(n.size) : 0]
        unset_wall(stack.last, np)
        visited[np]=true
        # if all neighbors are visited then there is
        # nothing left to do
        stack.pop if n.size==1
        stack.push np
      end
    end
    self
  end
end
```

This algorithm came out very cleanly, I think. Not a bit operation in sight. First it turns all the walls on. Then it sets up an Hash for tracking visited cells and a stack to drive the process. While there is something on the stack, the code looks at each not-yet-visited neighbor. If there are no neighbors in that set, the stack is popped, and the routine moves on. However, if there are, one is chosen at random, and the wall is knocked out between them. If that neighbor was the last unvisited one for this cell, the code pops the current cell off the stack. The neighbor cell is set to visited and pushed onto the stack, moving the build process to that location for the next iteration.

Solving a Maze

That covers creation. Now we need a solver:

code/amazing_mazes/fast_maze.rb

```ruby
class Maze
  # central part of Dijkstra's shortest path algorithm:
  # returns a hash that associates each reachable (from start) position
  # p, with the previous position on the shortest path from start to p
  # and the length of that path.
  # example: if the shortest path from 0 to 2 is [0, 1, 2], then
  # prev[2]==[1, 2], prev[1]==[0, 1] and prev[0]==[nil, 0].
  # so you can get all shortest paths from start to each reachable
  # position out of the returned hash.
  # if stop_at!=nil the method stops when the previous cell on the
  # shortest path from start to stop_at is found.
  def build_prev_hash(start, stop_at=nil)
    prev={start=>[nil, 0]} # hash to be returned
    return prev if stop_at==start
    # positions that we have seen, but we are not yet sure about
    # the shortest path to them (the value is length of the path,
    # for delete_min_value):
    active={start=>0}
    until active.empty?
      # get the position with the shortest path from the
      # active list
      cur=active.delete_min_value
      return prev if cur==stop_at
      newlength=prev[cur][1]+1 # path to cur length + 1
      # for all reachable neighbors of cur, check whether we found
      # a shorter path to them
      neighbors(cur).each { |n|
        # ignore unreachable
        next if wall_between?(cur, n)
        if old=prev[n] # was n already visited
          # if we found a longer path, ignore it
          next if newlength>=old[1]
        end
        # (re)add new position to active list
        active[n]=newlength
        # set new prev and length
        prev[n]=[cur, newlength]
      }
    end
    prev
  end
end
```

I really don't think I need to launch into too deep an explanation here because the comments guide you right through it. The short story is that this method branches out from a starting cell, walking to each

neighbor and always counting its steps. While doing this, it is building the Hash described in the first comment, which points to the cell
that came before on the shortest path. Using that Hash, returned by
this method, you can easily construct the shortest path to any cell the
algorithm visited. Handy stuff! Let's see how it gets put to use:

```
code/amazing_mazes/fast_maze.rb
class Maze
  def shortest_path(from, to)
    prev=build_prev_hash(from, to)
    if prev[to]
      # path found, build it by following the prev hash from
      # "to" to "from"
      path=[to]
      path.unshift(to) while to=prev[to][0]
      path
    else
      nil
    end
  end
end
```

Given a starting and ending cell, this returns just what the name
implies. It builds the magic Hash we looked at on the first line and
then just walks the path in reverse until it reaches the start (nil in the
Hash). Again, clean and simple. Nice coding, Dominik.

Let's look at the other search the code provides:

```
code/amazing_mazes/fast_maze.rb
class Maze
  # finds the longest shortest path in this maze, works only if there is
  # at least one position that can reach only one neighbor, because we
  # search only starting at those positions.
  def longest_shortest_path
    startp=endp=nil
    max=-1
    @wh.times { |p|
      # if current p can only reach 1 neighbor
      if neighbors(p).reject { |n| wall_between?(p, n) }.size==1
        prev=build_prev_hash(p)
        # search longest path from p
        tend, tmax=nil, -1
        prev.each { |k, v|
          if v[1]>tmax
            tend=k
            tmax=v[1]
          end
        }
        if tmax>max
```

```
            max=tmax
            startp, endp=p, tend
          end
        end
      }
      if startp # path found
        shortest_path(startp, endp)
      else
        nil
      end
    end
  end
end
```

This method walks the maze, looking for cells that are dead ends. From each of those, it builds the path Hash and checks the lengths of each path found. In the end, it will return the longest shortest path it found.

Interface

Just a little more code is needed for the human interface:

`code/amazing_mazes/fast_maze.rb`
```
if $0 == __FILE__
  ARGV.shift if search_longest=ARGV[0]=="-l"
  w, h, from, to=ARGV
  m=Maze.new(w.to_i, h.to_i)
  m.generate
  puts "Maze:", m.to_s
  if from=~/(\d+),(\d+)/
    p1=m.coord2pos($1.to_i, $2.to_i)
  else
    p1=rand(m.w*m.h)
  end
  if to=~/(\d+),(\d+)/
    p2=m.coord2pos($1.to_i, $2.to_i)
  else
    p2=rand(m.w*m.h)
  end

  path=m.shortest_path(p1, p2)
  puts "\nShortest path from #{m.pos2coord(p1).inspect} to " \
  "#{m.pos2coord(p2).inspect}:", m.to_s(path)

  if search_longest
    path=m.longest_shortest_path
    puts "\nLongest shortest path (from " \
    "#{m.pos2coord(path[0]).inspect} to " \
    "#{m.pos2coord(path[-1]).inspect}:",
    m.to_s(path)
  end
end
```

This is simply option parsing and displaying. The code checks for a special first -l option, which sets a flag to add the long search.

The next chunk reads a width and height and then builds and displays a maze of the indicated size. The code next reads from and to cells for a solution search, if they were provided. Random coordinates are used when from or to cells are absent. Note the use of the coord2pos() converter in here.

Finally, the shortest path is displayed. The longer search is also added, if requested. Dominik uses an unusual Ruby idiom here. Placing two string literals next to each other will cause Ruby to concatenate them, even without a + between them. (I didn't know this!) However, the rumor is that this feature may vanish in a future version of Ruby, so it's probably not a good technique to use.

Additional Exercises

1. Clifford Heath points out the following:

> Unfortunately, if you look at the mazes this algorithm generates, you'll see a serious flaw. They always seem to "fan out" from the start position—in other words, there is not a random nature to the shape of the paths away from the start position. It makes the mazes much easier to solve. I made the same mistake when I first wrote a maze generator.
>
> There is a commonly accepted alternative method (which produces "random" mazes).
>
> The idea is to start as Dominik did, with a maze having all walls intact—every cell has two intact walls so it's closed from every other cell. Every cell is numbered, say top-left to bottom-right, as in 0..(W×H-1). This number is known as the domain number, and every cell bearing a certain number is defined to be reachable from any cell in that domain.
>
> Whenever you break a wall separating two domains, you join them into one domain, because any cell in either domain can now reach any cell in the other domain. So to keep things intact, you must eliminate one domain by changing all occurrences of that number to the other one. I always eliminate the higher-numbered one, so the maze ends up as one domain numbered zero.
>
> Whenever you consider a wall you might want to break, check the domain numbers on either side. If they're the same, there is already a path between the two cells, and breaking this wall will

make a duplicate path, which is not what you want. If they're different, however, there is no path between the two cells, and it's OK to break this wall, eliminating one of the two domains.

The only remaining task is to find an efficient and random search for a wall to break. The easiest way is to choose a cell at random, check both walls (in random order), and if that wall divides two domains, break it. If not, consider the next cell (circular search) until you find a wall you can break.

As you have W×H cells, there are initially that many domains, and because every break reduces the domain count by one, you must break exactly W×H-1 walls to get to a maze where every cell is reachable from every other.

Try implementing this algorithm.

2. Modify your solution to allow a user to try to solve the maze interactively. The user should be able to enter the direction they want to go, and then the path can be extended in that direction. If the user backtracks, erase their abandoned steps.

Answer 22
From page 59

Learning Tic-Tac-Toe

The first thing any solution to this quiz is going to need is a few tools to manipulate tic-tac-toe positions. While they are really just a means to an end, the tools are interesting enough to warrant some discussion of their own. Here's my tic-tac-toe framework:

```
code/learning_tic_tac_toe/tictactoe.rb
module TicTacToe
  module SquaresContainer
    def []( index ) @squares[index] end

    def blanks()  @squares.find_all { |s| s == " " }.size end
    def os()      @squares.find_all { |s| s == "O" }.size end
    def xs()      @squares.find_all { |s| s == "X" }.size end
  end

  class Board
    class Row
      def initialize( squares, names )
        @squares  = squares
        @names    = names
      end

      include SquaresContainer

      def to_board_name( index )
        Board.index_to_name(@names[index])
      end
    end

    def self.name_to_index( name )
      x = name.gsub!(/([a-cA-C])/, "").to_i - 1
      y = ($1.downcase)[0] - ?a
      x + y * 3
    end
  end
```

```ruby
  def self.index_to_name( index )
    if index >= 6
      "c" + (index - 5).to_s
    elsif index >= 3
      "b" + (index - 2).to_s
    else
      "a" + (index + 1).to_s
    end
  end
end

def initialize( squares )
  @squares = squares
end

include SquaresContainer

def []( *indices )
  if indices.size == 2
    super indices[0] + indices[1] * 3
  elsif indices[0].is_a? Fixnum
    super indices[0]
  else
    super Board.name_to_index(indices[0].to_s)
  end
end

def each_row
  rows = [ [0, 1, 2], [3, 4, 5], [6, 7, 8],
      [0, 3, 6], [1, 4, 7], [2, 5, 8],
      [0, 4, 8], [2, 4, 6] ]
  rows.each do |e|
    yield Row.new(@squares.values_at(*e), e)
  end
end

def moves
  moves = [ ]
  @squares.each_with_index do |s, i|
    moves << Board.index_to_name(i) if s == " "
  end
  moves
end

def won?
  each_row do |row|
    return "X" if row.xs == 3
    return "O" if row.os == 3
  end
  return " " if blanks == 0
  false
end
```

```
    def to_s
      @squares.join
    end
  end
end
```

Breaking that code down, we see that our tools live in the TicTacToe namespace. The first of those is a mix-in module called SquaresContainer. It provides methods for indexing a given square and counting blanks, *X*s, and *O*s.

We then reach the definition of a TicTacToe::Board. This begins by defining a helper class called Row. Row accepts an array of squares and their corresponding board names or positions on the actual Board. It includes SquaresContainer, so we get access to all its methods. Finally, it defines a helper method, to_board_name(), you can use to ask Row what a given square would be called in the Board object.

Now we can actually dig into how Board works. It begins by creating class methods that translate between a chess-like square name (such as "b3") and the internal index representation.

We can see from initialize() that Board is just a collection of squares. We can also see, right under that, that it too includes SquaresContainer. However, Board overrides the ()() method to allow indexing by name, x and y indices, or a single 0 to 8 index.

Next we run into Board's primary iterator, each_row(). The method builds a list of all the Rows we care about in tic-tac-toe: three across, three down, and two diagonal. Then each of those Rows is **yield**ed to the provided block. This makes it easy to run some logic over the whole Board, Row by Row.

The moves() method returns a list of moves available. It does this by walking the list of squares and looking for blanks. It translates those to the prettier name notation as it finds them.

The next method, won?(), is an example of each_row() put to good use. It calls the iterator, passing a block that searches for three *X*s or *O*s. If it finds them, it returns the winner. Otherwise, it returns false. That allows it to be used in boolean tests and to find out who won a game.

Finally, to_s() just returns the Array of squares in String form.

The next thing we need are some players. Let's start that off with a base class:

```
code/learning_tic_tac_toe/tictactoe.rb
module TicTacToe
  class Player
    def initialize( pieces )
      @pieces = pieces
    end

    attr_reader :pieces

    def move( board )
      raise NotImplementedError, "Player subclasses must define move()."
    end

    def finish( final_board )
    end
  end
end
```

Player tracks, and provides an accessor for, the Player's pieces. It also defines move(), which subclasses must override to play the game, and finish(), which subclasses can override to see the end result of the game.

Using that, we can define a HumanPlayer with a terminal interface:

```
code/learning_tic_tac_toe/tictactoe.rb
module TicTacToe
  class HumanPlayer < Player
    def move( board )
      draw_board board

      moves = board.moves
      print "Your move?  (format: b3)   "
      move = $stdin.gets
      until moves.include?(move.chomp.downcase)
        print "Invalid move.  Try again.   "
        move = $stdin.gets
      end
      move
    end

    def finish( final_board )
      draw_board final_board

      if final_board.won? == @pieces
        print "Congratulations, you win.\n\n"
      elsif final_board.won? == " "
        print "Tie game.\n\n"
      else
        print "You lost tic-tac-toe?!\n\n"
      end
    end
```

```ruby
    private

    def draw_board( board )
      rows = [ [0, 1, 2], [3, 4, 5], [6, 7, 8] ]
      names = %w{a b c}
      puts
      print(rows.map do |r|
        names.shift + "  " + r.map { |e| board[e] }.join(" | ") + "\n"
      end.join("  --+--+--\n"))
      print "    1   2   3\n\n"
    end
  end
end
```

The move() method shows the board to the player and asks for a move. It loops until it has a valid move and then returns it. The other overridden method, finish(), displays the final board and explains who won. The private method draw_board() is the tool used by the other two methods to render a human-friendly board from Board.to_s().

Taking that a step further, let's build a couple of AI Players. These won't be legal solutions to the quiz, but they give us something to go on. Here are the classes:

`code/learning_tic_tac_toe/tictactoe.rb`

```ruby
module TicTacToe
  class DumbPlayer < Player
    def move( board )
      moves = board.moves
      moves[rand(moves.size)]
    end
  end

  class SmartPlayer < Player
    def move( board )
      moves = board.moves

      # If I have a win, take it.  If he is threatening to win, stop it.
      board.each_row do |row|
        if row.blanks == 1 and (row.xs == 2 or row.os == 2)
          (0..2).each do |e|
            return row.to_board_name(e) if row[e] == " "
          end
        end
      end

      # Take the center if open.
      return "b2" if moves.include? "b2"
```

```
    # Defend opposite corners.
    if board[0] != @pieces and board[0] != " " and board[8] == " "
      return "c3"
    elsif board[8] != @pieces and board[8] != " " and board[0] == " "
      return "a1"
    elsif board[2] != @pieces and board[2] != " " and board[6] == " "
      return "c1"
    elsif board[6] != @pieces and board[6] != " " and board[2] == " "
      return "a3"
    end


    # Defend against the special case XOX on a diagonal.
    if board.xs == 2 and board.os == 1 and board[4] == "O" and
       (board[0] == "X" and board[8] == "X") or
       (board[2] == "X" and board[6] == "X")
      return %w{a2 b1 b3 c2}[rand(4)]
    end


    # Or make a random move.
    moves[rand(moves.size)]
      end
    end
  end
end
```

The first AI, DumbPlayer, just chooses random moves from the legal choices. It has no knowledge of the games, but it doesn't learn anything either.

The other AI, SmartPlayer, can play stronger tic-tac-toe. Note that this implementation is a little unusual. Traditionally, tic-tac-toe is solved on a computer with a *minimax* search. The idea behind minimax is that your opponent will always choose the best, or "maximum," move. Given that, we don't need to concern ourselves with obviously dumb moves. While looking over the opponent's best move, we can choose the least, or "minimum," damaging move to our cause and head for that. Though vital to producing something like a strong chess player, minimax always seems like overkill for tic-tac-toe. I took the easy way out and distilled my own tic-tac-toe knowledge into a few tests to create SmartPlayer.

The final class we need for tic-tac-toe is a Game class:

```
code/learning_tic_tac_toe/tictactoe.rb
module TicTacToe
  class Game
    def initialize( player1, player2, random = true )
      if random and rand(2) == 1
        @x_player = player2.new("X")
        @o_player = player1.new("O")
```

```ruby
      else
        @x_player = player1.new("X")
        @o_player = player2.new("O")
      end

      @board = Board.new([" "] * 9)
    end

    attr_reader :x_player, :o_player

    def play
      until @board.won?
        update_board @x_player.move(@board), @x_player.pieces
        break if @board.won?

        update_board @o_player.move(@board), @o_player.pieces
      end

      @o_player.finish @board
      @x_player.finish @board
    end

    private

    def update_board( move, piece )
      m = Board.name_to_index(move)
      @board = Board.new((0..8).map { |i| i == m ? piece : @board[i] })
    end
  end
end
```

The constructor for Game takes two factory objects that can produce the desired subclasses of Player. This is a common technique in object-oriented programming, but Ruby makes it trivial, because classes are objects—you simply pass the Class objects to the method. Instances of those classes are assigned to instance variables after randomly deciding who goes first, if random is **true**. Otherwise, they are assigned in the passed order. The last step is to create a Board with nine empty squares.

The play() method runs an entire game, start to finish, alternating moves until a winner is found. The private update_board() method makes this possible by replacing the Board instance variable with each move.

It's trivial to turn that into a playable game:

```
code/learning_tic_tac_toe/tictactoe.rb
if __FILE__ == $0
  if ARGV.size > 0 and ARGV[0] == "-d"
    ARGV.shift
    game = TicTacToe::Game.new TicTacToe::HumanPlayer,
                  TicTacToe::DumbPlayer
  else
    game = TicTacToe::Game.new TicTacToe::HumanPlayer,
                  TicTacToe::SmartPlayer
  end
  game.play
end
```

That builds a Game and calls play(). It defaults to using a SmartPlayer, but you can request a DumbPlayer with the -d command-line switch.

Enough playing around with tic-tac-toe. We now have what we need to solve the quiz. How do we "learn" the game? Let's look to history for the answer.

The History of MENACE

This quiz was inspired by the research of Donald Michie. In 1961 he built a "machine" that learned to play perfect tic-tac-toe against humans, using matchboxes and beads. He called the machine MENACE (Matchbox Educable Naughts And Crosses Engine). Here's how he did it.

More than 300 matchboxes were labeled with images of tic-tac-toe positions and filled with colored beads representing possible moves. At each move, a bead would be rattled out of the proper box to determine a move. When MENACE would win, more beads of the colors played would be added to each position box. When it would lose, the beads were left out to discourage these moves.

Michie claimed that he trained MENACE in 220 games. That sounds promising, so let's update MENACE to modern-day Ruby.

Filling a Matchbox Brain

First, we need to map out all the positions of tic-tac-toe. We'll store those in an external file so we can reload them as needed. What format shall we use for the file, though? I say Ruby itself. We can just store some constructor calls inside an Array and call eval() to reload as needed.

Here's the start of my solution code:

```
code/learning_tic_tac_toe/menace.rb
require "tictactoe"

class MENACE < TicTacToe::Player
  class Position
    def self.generate_positions( io )
      io << "[\n"
      queue = [self.new]
      queue[-1].save(io)

      seen = [queue[-1]]
      while queue.size > 0
        positions = queue.shift.leads_to.
                       reject { |p| p.over? or seen.include?(p) }
        positions.each { |p| p.save(io) } if positions.size > 0 and
                                      positions[0].turn == "X"
        queue.push(*positions)
        seen.push(*positions)
      end
      io << "]\n"
    end
  end
end
```

You can see that MENACE begins by defining a class to hold Positions. The class method generate_positions() walks the entire tree of possible tic-tac-toe moves with the help of leads_to(). This is really just a breadth-first search looking for all possible endings. We do keep track of what we have seen before, though, because there is no sense in examining a Position and the Positions resulting from it twice.

Note that only *X*-move positions are mapped. The original MENACE always played *X*, and to keep things simple I've kept that convention here.

You can see that this method writes the Array delimiters to io, before and after the Position search. The save() method that is called during the search will fill in the contents of the previously discussed Ruby source file format.

Let's see those methods generate_positions() is depending on:

```
code/learning_tic_tac_toe/menace.rb
class MENACE < TicTacToe::Player
  class Position
    def initialize( box   = TicTacToe::Board.new([" "] * 9),
                    beads = (0..8).to_a * 4 )
      @box   = box
      @beads = beads
    end
```

```ruby
def leads_to(   )
  @box.moves.inject([ ]) do |all, move|
    m       = TicTacToe::Board.name_to_index(move)
    box     = TicTacToe::Board.new((0..8).
              map { |i| i == m ? turn : @box[i] })
    beads = @beads.reject { |b| b == m }
    if turn == "O"
      i = beads.rindex(beads[0])
      beads = beads[0...i] unless i == 0
    end
    all << self.class.new(box, beads)
  end
end

def over?(   )
  @box.moves.size == 1 or @box.won?
end

def save( io )
  box     = @box.to_s.split("").map { |c| %Q{"#{c}"} }.join(", ")
  beads = @beads.inspect

  io << "    MENACE::Position.new([#{box}], #{beads}),\n"
end

def turn(   )
  if @box.xs == @box.os then "X" else "O" end
end

def box_str(   )
  @box.to_s
end

def ==( other )
  box_str == other.box_str
end
    end
  end
```

If you glance at initialize(), you'll see that a Position is really just a match-box and some beads. The tic-tac-toe framework provides the means to draw positions on the box, and beads are an Array of Integer indices.

The leads_to() method returns all Positions reachable from the current setup. It uses the tic-tac-toe framework to walk all possible moves. After pulling the beads out to pay for the move, the new box and beads are wrapped in a Position of their own and added to the results. This does involve knowledge of tic-tac-toe, but it's used only to build MENACE's memory map. It could be done by hand.

Obviously, over?() starts returning true as soon as anyone has won the game. Less obvious, though, is that over?() is used to prune last move positions as well. We don't need to map positions where we have no choices.

The save() method handles marshaling the data to a Ruby format. My implementation is simple and will have a trailing comma for the final element in the Array. Ruby allows this, for this very reason. Handy, eh?

The turn() method is a helper used to get the current player's symbol, and the last two methods just define equality between positions. Two positions are considered equal if their boxes show the same board setup.

```
code/learning_tic_tac_toe/menace.rb
class MENACE < TicTacToe::Player
  class Position
    def learn_win( move )
      return if @beads.size == 1
      2.times { @beads << move }
    end

    def learn_loss( move )
      return if @beads.size == 1
      @beads.delete_at(@beads.index(move))
      @beads.uniq! if @beads.uniq.size == 1
    end

    def choose_move(  )
      @beads[rand(@beads.size)]
    end
  end
end
```

The other interesting methods in Position are learn_win() and learn_loss(). When a position is part of a win, we add two more beads for the selected move. When it's part of a loss, we remove the bead that caused the mistake. Draws have no effect. That's how MENACE learns.

Flowing naturally from that we have choose_move(), which randomly selects a bead. That represents the best of MENACE's collected knowledge about this Position.

Ruby's MENACE

Let's examine the player itself:

```
code/learning_tic_tac_toe/menace.rb
class MENACE < TicTacToe::Player
  BRAIN_FILE = "brain.rb"
  unless test(?e, BRAIN_FILE)
    File.open(BRAIN_FILE, "w") { |file| Position.generate_positions(file) }
  end
  BRAIN = File.open(BRAIN_FILE, "r") { |file| eval(file.read) }

  def initialize( pieces )
    super

    @moves = []
  end

  def move( board )
    choices = board.moves
    return choices[0] if choices.size == 1

    current  = Position.new(board, [ ])
    position = BRAIN.find() { |p| p == current }

    move = position.choose_move
    @moves << [position, move]
    TicTacToe::Board.index_to_name(move)
  end

  def finish( final_board )
    if final_board.won? == @pieces
      @moves.each { |(pos, move)| pos.learn_win(move) }
    elsif final_board.won? != " "
      @moves.each { |(pos, move)| pos.learn_loss(move) }
    end
  end
end
```

MENACE uses the constant BRAIN to contain its knowledge. If BRAIN_FILE doesn't exist, it is created. In either case, it's eval()ed to produce BRAIN. Building the brain file can take a few minutes, but it needs to be done only once. If you want to see how to speed it up, look at the *Joe Asks* box on the next page.

The rest of MENACE is a trivial three-step process: initialize() starts keeping track of all our moves for this game, move() shakes a bead out of the box, and finish() ensures we learn from our wins and losses.

We can top that off with a simple "main" program to create a game:

Joe Asks...
Three Hundred Positions?

I said that Donald Michie used a little more than 300 match-boxes. Then I went on to build a solution that uses 2,201. What's the deal?

Michie trimmed the positions needed with a few tricks. Turning the board 90 degrees doesn't change the position any, and we could do that up to three times. *Mirroring* the board, swapping the top and bottom rows, is a similar harmless change. Then we could rotate that mirrored board up to three times. All of these changes reduce the positions to consider, but it does complicate the solution to work them in.

There are rewards for the work, though. Primarily, MENACE would learn faster with this approach, because it wouldn't have to learn the same position in multiple formats.

code/learning_tic_tac_toe/menace.rb

```ruby
if __FILE__ == $0
  puts "Training..."
  if ARGV.size == 1 and ARGV[0] =~ /^\d+$/
    ARGV[0].to_i.times do
      game = TicTacToe::Game.new(MENACE, TicTacToe::SmartPlayer, false)
      game.play
    end
  end

  play_again = true
  while play_again
    game = TicTacToe::Game.new(MENACE, TicTacToe::HumanPlayer, false)
    game.play

    print "Play again?   "
    play_again = $stdin.gets =~ /^y/i
  end
end
```

The command-line argument is the number of times to train MENACE against SmartPlayer. After, you can play interactive games against the machine. I suggest 10,000 training games and then playing with the machine a bit. It won't be perfect yet, but it will be starting to learn. Try catching it out the same way until you see it learn to avoid the mistake.

Additional Exercises

1. Implement MinimaxPlayer.

2. Shrink the positions listing using rotations and mirroring.

3. Adapt MENACE to retain its knowledge between runs.

4. Adapt MENACE to show when it has mastered the game.

Countdown

At first glance, the search space for this problem looks very large. The six source numbers can be ordered various ways, and you don't have to use all the numbers. Beyond that, you can have one of four operators between each pair of numbers. Finally, consider that 1 * 2 + 3 is different from 1 * (2 + 3). That's a lot of combinations.

However, we can prune that large search space significantly. Let's start with some simple examples and work our way up. Addition and multiplication are commutative, so we have this:

```
1 + 2 = 3 and 2 + 1 = 3
1 * 2 = 2 and 2 * 1 = 2
```

We don't need to handle it both ways. One will do.

Moving on to numbers, the example in the quiz used two 5s as source numbers. Obviously, these two numbers are interchangeable. The first 5 plus 2 is 7, just as the second 5 plus 2 is 7.

What about the possible source number 1? Anything times 1 is itself, so there is no need to check multiplication of 1. Similarly, anything divided by 1 is itself. No need to divide by 1.

Let's look at 0. Adding and subtracting 0 is pointless. Multiplying by 0 takes us back to 0, which is pretty far from a number from 100 to 999 (our goal). Dividing 0 by anything is the same story, and dividing by 0 is illegal, of course. Conclusion: 0 is useless. Now, you can't get 0 as a source number; but, you can safely ignore any operation(s) that result in 0.

Those are all single-number examples, of course. Time to think bigger. What about negative numbers? Our goal is somewhere from 100 to

999. Negative numbers are going the wrong way. They don't help, so you can safely ignore any operation that results in a negative number.

Finally, consider this:

```
(5 + 5) / 2 = 5
```

The previous is just busywork. We already had a 5; we didn't need to make one. Any operations that result in one of their operands can be ignored.

Using simplifications like the previous, you can get the search space down to something that can be brute-force searched pretty quickly, as long as we're dealing only with six numbers.

Pruning Code

Dennis Ranke submitted the most complete example of pruning, so let's start with that. Here's the code:

```ruby
code/countdown/pruning.rb
class Solver
  class Term
    attr_reader :value, :mask

    def initialize(value, mask, op = nil, left = nil, right = nil)
      @value = value
      @mask = mask
      @op = op
      @left = left
      @right = right
    end

    def to_s
      return @value.to_s unless @op
      "(#@left #@op #@right)"
    end
  end

  def initialize(sources, target)
    printf "%s -> %d\n", sources.inspect, target
    @target = target
    @new_terms = []
    @num_sources = sources.size
    @num_hashes = 1 << @num_sources

    # the hashes are used to check for duplicate terms
    # (terms that have the same value and use the same
    # source numbers)
    @term_hashes = Array.new(@num_hashes) { {} }
```

```
      # enter the source numbers as (simple) terms
      sources.each_with_index do |value, index|

        # each source number is represented by one bit in the bit mask
        mask = 1 << index
        p mask
        p value
        term = Term.new(value, mask)
        @new_terms << term
        @term_hashes[mask][value] = term
      end
    end
  end
end
```

The Term class is easy enough. It is used to build tree-like representations of math operations. A Term can be a single number or @left Term, @right Term, and the @op joining them. The @value of such a Term would be the result of performing that math.

The tricky part in this solution is that it uses bit masks to compare Terms. The mask is just a collection of bit switches used to represent the source numbers. The bits correspond to the index for that source number. You can see this being set up right at the bottom of initialize().

These mask-to-Term pairs get stored in @term_hashes. This variable holds an Array, which will be indexed with the mask of source numbers in a Term. For example, an index mask of 0b000101 (5 in decimal) means that the first and third source numbers are used, which are index 0 and 2 in both the binary mask and the source list.

Inside the Array, each index holds a Hash. Those Hashes hold decimal value to Term pairs. The values are numbers calculated by combining Terms. For example, if our first source number is 100 and the second is 2, the Hash at Array index 0b000011 (3) will eventually hold the keys 50, 98, 102, and 200. The values for these will be the Term objects showing the operators needed to produce the number.

All of this bit twiddling is very memory efficient. It takes a lot less computer memory to store 0b000011 than it does [100, 2].

`code/countdown/pruning.rb`

```
class Solver
  def run
    collision = 0
    best_difference = 1.0/0.0
    next_new_terms = [nil]
    until next_new_terms.empty?
      next_new_terms = []
```

```ruby
# temporary hashes for terms found in this iteration
# (again to check for duplicates)
new_hashes = Array.new(@num_hashes) { {} }

# iterate through all the new terms (those that weren't yet used
# to generate composite terms)
@new_terms.each do |term|

  # iterate through the hashes and find those containing terms
  # that share no source numbers with 'term'
  index = 1
  term_mask = term.mask

  # skip over indices that clash with term_mask
  index += collision - ((collision - 1) & index) while
          (collision = term_mask & index) != 0
  while index < @num_hashes
    hash = @term_hashes[index]

    # iterate through the hashes and build composite terms using
    # the four basic operators
    hash.each_value do |other|
      new_mask = term_mask | other.mask
      hash = @term_hashes[new_mask]
      new_hash = new_hashes[new_mask]

      # sort the source terms so that the term with the larger
      # value is left
      # (we don't allow fractions and negative subterms are not
      # necessairy as long as the target is positive)
      if term.value > other.value
        left_term = term
        right_term = other
      else
        left_term = other
        right_term = term
      end
      [:+, :-, :*, :/].each do |op|

        # don't allow fractions
        next if op == :/ &&
                left_term.value % right_term.value != 0

        # calculate value of composite term
        value = left_term.value.send(op, right_term.value)

        # don't allow zero
        next if value == 0

        # ignore this composite term if this value was already
```

```
      # found for a different term using the same source
      # numbers
      next if hash.has_key?(value) || new_hash.has_key?(value)

      new_term = Term.new(value, new_mask, op, left_term,
                          right_term)

      # if the new term is closer to the target than the
      # best match so far print it out
      if (value - @target).abs < best_difference
        best_difference = (value - @target).abs
        printf "%s = %d (error: %d)\n", new_term, value,
                          best_difference
        return if best_difference == 0
      end

      # remember the new term for use in the next iteration
      next_new_terms << new_term
      new_hash[value] = new_term
    end
  end
  index += 1
  index += collision - ((collision - 1) & index) while
            (collision = term_mask & index) != 0
    end
  end

  # merge the hashes with the new terms into the main hashes
  @term_hashes.each_with_index do |hash, index|
    hash.merge!(new_hashes[index])
  end

  # the newly found terms will be used in the next iteration
  @new_terms = next_new_terms
    end
  end
end
```

That's very well-commented code, so I won't bother to break it all down.
I do want to point out a few things, though.

This method repeatedly walks through all of the @new_terms, combining
them with all the already found @term_hashes to reach new values. At
each step we build up a collection of next_new_terms that will replace
@new_terms when the process loops. Also being loaded is new_hashes,
which will be merged into @term_hashes, giving us more to expand on in
the next iteration.

Be sure to spot the two pieces of code for avoiding collisions. If we
find ourselves working with an index that matches the term_mask at any

point, we know we are duplicating work because we are working with the same source list. In these cases, index gets bumped to move us along.

The rest of the method is the pruning work we looked into at the start of this discussion. The comments will point out what each section of code is skipping.

Here's the code you need to turn all that work into a solution:

```
code/countdown/pruning.rb
if ARGV[0] && ARGV[0].downcase == 'random'
  ARGV[0] = rand(900) + 100
  ARGV[1] = (rand(4) + 1) * 25
  5.times {|i| ARGV[i + 2] = rand(10) + 1}
end

if ARGV.size < 3
  puts "Usage: ruby #$0 <target> <source1> <source2> ..."
  puts "   or: ruby #$0 random"
  exit
end

start_time = Time.now
Solver.new(ARGV[1..-1].map {|v| v.to_i}, ARGV[0].to_i).run
printf "%f seconds\n", Time.now - start_time
```

The previous solution is lightning fast. Run it a few times to see for yourself. It can work so fast because heavy pruning allows it to skip a lot of useless operations.

Coding Different Strategies

Next, I want to look at Brian Schröder's solution. I won't show the whole thing here because it's quite a lot of code. However, it can switch solving methods as directed and even solve using fractions. Here's the heart of it:

```
code/countdown/countdown.rb
# Search all possible terms for the ones that fit best.

# Systematically create all terms over all subsets of the set of numbers in
# source, and find the one that is closest to target.
#
# Returns the solution that is closest to the target.
#
# If a block is given, calls the block each time a better or equal solution
# is found.
#
# As a heuristic to guide the search, sort the numbers ascending.
```

```ruby
def solve_countdown(target, source, use_module)
  source = source.sort_by{|i|-i}
  best = nil
  best_distance = 1.0/0.0
  use_module::each_term_over(source) do | term |
    distance = (term.value - target).abs
    if distance <= best_distance
      best_distance = distance
      best = term
      yield best if block_given?
    end
  end
  return best
end
```

This method takes the target and source numbers in addition to a Module (which I'll return to in a minute) as parameters. The first line is the sort mentioned in the comment. Then best and best_distance are initialized to nil and infinity (1.0/0.0) to track the best solution discovered so far.

After the setup, the method calls into the each_term_over() method, provided by the Module it was called with. The Module to use is determined by the interface code (not shown) based on the provided command-line switches. There are four possible choices. Two deal with fractions while two are integer only, and there is a recursive and "memoized" version for each number type. The program switches solving strategies based on the user's requests. (This is a nice use of the Strategy design pattern.)

Here is each_term_over() in the ModuleRecursive::Integral:

code/countdown/countdown-recursive.rb
```ruby
module Recursive
  # Allow only integral results
  module Integral
    # Call the given block for each term that can be constructed over a set
    # of numbers.
    #
    # Recursive implementation that calls a block each time a new term has been
    # stitched together. Returns each term multiple times.
    #
    # This version checks that only integral results may result.
    #
    # Here I explicitly coded the operators, because there is not
    # much redundance.
    #
    # This may be a bit slow, because it zips up through the whole callstack
    # each time a new term is created.
```

```ruby
def Integral.each_term_over(source)
  if source.length == 1
    yield source[0]
  else
    source.each_partition do | p1, p2 |
      each_term_over(p1) do | op1 |
        yield op1
        each_term_over(p2) do | op2 |
          yield op2
          if op2.value != 0
            yield Term.new(op1, op2, :+)
            yield Term.new(op1, op2, :-)
            yield Term.new(op1, op2, :'/') if op2.value != 1 and
                                              op1.value % op2.value == 0
          end
          if op1.value != 0
            yield Term.new(op2, op1, :-)
            if op1.value != 1
              yield Term.new(op2, op1, :'/') if op2.value % op1.value == 0
              yield Term.new(op1, op2, :*) if op2.value != 0 and
                                             op2.value != 1
            end
          end
        end
      end
    end
  end
end
```

This method recursively generates terms in every possible combination. This is a key point to a working solution. If you try adding a number at a time, you generate solutions looking like these:

```
(((num op num) op num) op num)...
```

A tricky example posted to Ruby Talk by daz, "Target: 926, Source: 75, 2, 8, 5, 10, 10," shows off the folly of this approach. The only answer is the following:

```
(75 - 5 + 8) * (2 + 10) - 10
```

As you can see, the 2 + 10 term must be built separately from the 75 - 5 + 8 term, and then the two can be combined.

Getting back to the previous code, the each_partition() method it uses was added to Array in a different section of the code (not shown). It returns "each true partition (containing no empty set) exactly once."

Term objects (not shown) just manage their operands and operator, providing mainly String representation and result evaluation.

The block we're yielding to is the block passed by solve_countdown(), which we examined earlier. It simply keeps track of the best solution generated so far.

The interesting part of all this is the same method in a different module. The listing on the next page is the each_term_over() method from Memoized::Integral.

The result of this method is the same, but it uses a technique called *memoization* to work faster. When Terms are generated in here, they get added to the Hash memo. After that, all the magic is in the very first line, which simply skips all the work the next time those source numbers are examined.

This trades memory (the Hash of stored results) for speed (no repeat work). That's why the solution provides other options too. Maybe the target platform won't have the memory to spare. This is a handy technique showcased in a nice implementation.

Additional Exercises

1. Try adding some pruning or memoization to your solution. Time solving the same problem before and afterward to see if whether speeds up the search.

2. You can find a great web-based interactive solver for this number game at http://www.crosswordtools.com/numbers-game/. Extend your solution to provide a similar web interface.

```
code/countdown/countdown-memoized.rb
module Memoized
  module Integral
    # Call the given block for each term that can be constructed over
    # a set of numbers.
    #
    # Recursive implementation that calls a block each time a new term
    # has been stitched together.  Returns each term multiple times.
    #
    # This version checks that only integral results may result.
    #
    # Here I explicitly coded the operators, because there is not much
    # redundancy.
    #
    # This may be a bit slow, because it zips up through the whole
    # callstack each time a new term is created.
    def Integral.each_term_over(source, memo = {}, &block)
      return memo[source] if memo[source]

      result = []
      if source.length == 1
        result << source[0]
      else
        source.each_partition do | p1, p2 |
          each_term_over(p1, memo, &block).each do | op1 |
            each_term_over(p2, memo, &block).each do | op2 |
              if op2.value != 0
                result << Term.new(op1, op2, :+)
                result << Term.new(op1, op2, :-)
                result << Term.new(op1, op2, :'/') if op2.value != 1 and
                                                      op1.value % op2.value == 0
              end
              if op1.value != 0
                result << Term.new(op2, op1, :-)
                if op1.value != 1
                  result << Term.new(op2, op1, :'/') if op2.value %
                                                        op1.value == 0
                  result << Term.new(op1, op2, :*) if op2.value != 0 and
                                                      op2.value != 1
                end
              end
            end
          end
        end
      end

      result.each do | term | block.call(term) end
      memo[source] = result
    end
  end
end
```

Answer **24**
From page 63

Solving Tactics

Tactics is a strange game to us chess players. I'm so used to considering going first to be an advantage that I was just sure it would be true here too. Wrong again. In Tactics, the second player can always force a win.

Though "why" this is true was part of the quiz, it hasn't really been answered to my satisfaction. I suspect it has to do with the moves remaining. The first player starts with the lead. The second player can always choose to respond with moves that keep the first player in the lead. If you're in the lead at the end of the game, you lose. Put another way, the second player can always add to the first player's move just the right amount of squares to keep the number of remaining moves optimal.

We can take that a step further and prove it with code. What you're really looking for in Tactics is a chance to leave the opponent with a single square to move in. When that opportunity comes, you can seize it and win. Until then, you want to try to make sure two moves, at minimum, are left. That ensures you will get another turn and another shot at the win. We can translate that to Ruby pretty easily, but first we need a way to store positions.

A couple of people, including myself, posted about our failed attempts to build the entire move tree as some complex data structure. You need to be a bit more clever than that. The key optimization is realizing that all squares are either on or off, thus ideal bit representation material. An empty board is just 0b0000_0000_0000_0000 and the final board is 0b1111_1111_1111_1111. To make a move, just OR (|) it to the board. To see whether a move is possible, AND (&) it to the board, and check for a result of zero (nonzero values shared some bits, so there were already pieces on those squares).

Let's see whether we can put that together to generate a move list:

```
code/solving_tactics/perfect_play.rb
class TacticsPosition
  MOVES = [ ]
  # a quick hack to load all possible moves (idea from Bob Sidebotham)
  (0..3).each do |row|
    # take all the moves available in one row...
    [ 0b1000, 0b0100, 0b0010, 0b0001, 0b1100,
      0b0110, 0b0011, 0b1110, 0b0111, 0b1111 ].each do |move|
      # spread it to each row of the board...
      move = move << 4 * row
      MOVES << move
      # and transpose it to the columns too
      MOVES << (0..15).inject(0) do |trans, i|
        q, r = i.divmod(4);
        trans |= move[i] << q + r * 4
      end
    end
  end
  MOVES.uniq!
end
```

The first thing I needed was a list of all possible moves. If we view the entire board as one long set of bit switches representing whether a piece is present, a move is just a group of consecutive bits to flip on. The good news is that we can generate all the moves from one row of moves, as the comments show us here.

Now I'm ready to flesh out a position class:

```
code/solving_tactics/perfect_play.rb
class TacticsPosition
  def initialize( position = 0b0000_0000_0000_0000, player = :first )
    @position = position
    @player   = player
  end

  include Enumerable

  # passes the new position after each available move to the block
  def each( &block )
    moves.map do |m|
      TacticsPosition.new(@position | m, next_player)
    end.each(&block)
  end

  def moves
    MOVES.reject { |m| @position & m != 0 }
  end
```

```ruby
def next_player
    if @player == :first then :second else :first end
  end
end
```

Each TacticsPosition object stores a single board position. Internally, these are managed as a single Integer using bit math.

TacticsPosition objects are Enumerable, allowing you to walk the next positions that can be reached from legal moves. As you can see, moves() are found by ANDing the board with all possible MOVES and tossing out anything that doesn't equal zero.

Finally, next_player() is just a helper method used by each() to flip-flop the player in new positions.

Let's get to playing:

`code/solving_tactics/perfect_play.rb`
```ruby
class TacticsPosition
  # the minimum number of plays left from this position
  def minimum_moves_left
    minimum = 0
    game = self
    until game.over?
      game = game.min { |a, b| a.moves.size <=> b.moves.size }
      minimum += 1
    end
    return minimum
  end

  # select a perfect move from this position, returning the resulting position
  def perfect_play
    win = find { |m| m.moves.size == 1 }
    if win      # if we can force a win, do so...
      win
    else        # otherwise, try to ensure at least two more moves
      choices = to_a.sort_by { |m| m.minimum_moves_left }
      best = choices.find { |m| m.moves.size % 2 == 0 }
      best or choices.first
    end
  end

  def over?
    @position == 0b1111_1111_1111_1111
  end
end
```

The real magic here is the combination of minimum_moves_left() and perfect_play(). You can see that the latter is almost a direct translation of the strategy I outlined previously. To do that, perfect_play() is relying on answers from minimum_move_left(), always keeping the move count optimal. minimum_moves_left() uses over?() to decide whether it can stop counting, which is simply when the board is completely full of pieces.

We just need a couple of helper methods to finish off this class:

```
code/solving_tactics/perfect_play.rb
class TacticsPosition
  # pretty display for humans (no bits!)
  def to_s
    board = "%016b" % @position
    board.tr!("01", "_X").gsub!("", " ").strip!
    board.gsub!(/(?:[X_] ){4}/, "\\&\n")

    if @position == 0b0000_0000_0000_0000
      "\n#{board}"
    else
      "\nThe #{next_player} player moves:\n\n#{board}\n\n"
    end
  end

  def winner
    @player
  end
end
```

This code builds up a display string by translating the @position integer to a string of 0s and 1s, swapping those with *X*s and blank squares, and finally inserting whitespace to break things up. The use of next_player() is a little tricky here—next_player() is also the last player, so we use it here to find who just moved.

If you run this solution, you will see that it gets the right answer. Assuming there is no flaw in my perfect-play strategy, the previous does represent a valid solution to the quiz. The challenge here is the proof of the strategy, which could be quite tricky. Let's move on to some solutions that use less knowledge of the game and see whether we can find our proof.

From Playing to Solving

If you want to solve the quiz without any outside math or strategy help, you'll need some form of search. That can get tricky, though. As Bob Sidebotham said in the README of his solution, there are 2^{16} (65,536) possible positions. Luckily, bits are fast and efficient, so they allow us to traverse the space quickly.

One solution (not shown), by Sea&Gull, was built from the logic that a 4×4 board would provide the same results as a 4×2 board. Solving that cut the search space severely, and the solution got the right answer. The burden there is proving the boards are indeed equal. That's the same problem we had before, so we will have to keep looking.

Bob Sidebotham came up with the solution that answers the quiz question to my satisfaction. We will get to exactly how he did that in just a moment, but first we need to see his Tactics library:

`code/solving_tactics/tactics.rb`

```ruby
class Tactics
  # The tactics board is represented as a 16-bit integer,
  # 0s representing empty square; 1s representing filled squares.
  EMPTY, FULL = 0, 0xFFFF

  # Record a WIN or LOSS for potentially each of the 2**16 possible
  # board positions. A position is recorded as a WIN (or LOSS) if
  # that position represents a WIN (or LOSS) to a player prior to
  # moving from that position.
  WIN, LOSS = 1, 0
  (@@position = Array.new(0x10000))[FULL] = WIN

  # Create a new Tactics game, starting at the specified position.
  def initialize(board = EMPTY, possible_moves = Tactics.all_possible_moves)
    @board = board
    @possible_moves = prune_possible_moves(board, possible_moves)
  end

  # Play from the current position. If *any* move guarantees a win,
  # then mark this position as a WIN and return it. Otherwise this
  # position loses.
  def play
    @possible_moves.each do |move|
      new_board = @board | move
      if ( @@position[new_board] ||
           Tactics.new(new_board, @possible_moves).play ) == LOSS then
        return @@position[@board] = WIN
      end
    end
    @@position[@board] = LOSS
  end

  private

  # Reduce the set of possible moves provided to the actual moves
  # that are possible from the specified starting position.
  def prune_possible_moves(board, possible_moves)
    possible_moves.reject { |move| (board & move) != 0 }
  end
```

```ruby
    # Compute all possible moves from an empty board.
  def self.all_possible_moves
      # Replicate the possibilities for a single row over each row and column of
      # the grid.
      (0..3).inject([]) do |moves, row|
        [ 0b1000, 0b0100, 0b0010, 0b0001, 0b1100,
          0b0110, 0b0011, 0b1110, 0b0111, 0b1111 ].each do |bits|
          move = bits << 4 * row
          moves << move << transpose(move)
        end
        moves
      end.uniq
  end

    # Return the transposed board (horizontal to vertical, or vice versa)
  def self.transpose(board)
      (0..15).inject(0) { |xboard, i|
        q,r = i.divmod(4); xboard |= board[i] << q + r*4
      }
  end
  end
end
```

I'm not going to insult everyone's intelligence by breaking down well-commented code, but I do want to point out a few things. Toward the top the constant FULL is set to 0xFFFF. This is just another way to say 0b1111_1111_1111_1111, which I mentioned earlier. On the second line of play(), you can see moves being made with |. prune_possible_moves() uses & and the check for zero to see what's possible at a given position. That should all be very familiar from the earlier solution.

The other point of interest is play(). Bob decided to work backward. It's easy to identify a win at the end of the game. Leave your opponent with only one square, as we discussed earlier. Expanding on that, any move that has a play leading to a position where you can leave the opponent stranded is also a win, because you will obviously make those two forced-win moves. We can keep walking that backward. Any position leading to those described is a win. And so on. Now if you don't have that sequence of forced moves, your opponent does, by simple logic. Anything that's a loss for you is a win for the opponent. If we take that all the way back to the first move, we can find the forced win and which side has it.

That's an exhaustive search, but thanks to the relatively small search space and the efficiency of our bit representation, we can afford to check everything. In fact, Bob's code needs only a little more than two seconds to find the answer on my box. Here's how he does it:

```
code/solving_tactics/whowins.rb
```
```ruby
require 'tactics'

puts %(#{Tactics.new.play == Tactics::WIN ? "First" : "Second"} player wins.)
```

Obviously, that just calls play(), triggering the exhaustive search we
just examined. I'm not done showing off Bob yet, though. He provided
another system of proof with his code.

Proof through Unit Testing

Have a look at this beautiful set of unit tests:

```
code/solving_tactics/tactics_test.rb
```
```ruby
require 'test/unit'
require 'tactics.rb'

class TestTactics < Test::Unit::TestCase
  # Test the play engine by trying various board positions that we
  # know are winning or losing positions. Each of these is justified
  # (no point in using ones that are just hunches on our part-'cause
  # then what would we be verifying?).
  def test_play
    # Each position description is the position you're faced with
    # just before playing. So "1 square loses" means that if it's
    # your turn to play and there's only one square available,
    # you lose.

    # 1 square loses (obviously)
    assert_equal(Tactics::LOSS, Tactics.new(0b0111_1111_1111_1111).play)
    assert_equal(Tactics::LOSS, Tactics.new(0b1011_1111_1111_1111).play)
    assert_equal(Tactics::LOSS, Tactics.new(0b1101_1111_1111_1111).play)
    assert_equal(Tactics::LOSS, Tactics.new(0b1110_1111_1111_1111).play)
    assert_equal(Tactics::LOSS, Tactics.new(0b1111_0111_1111_1111).play)
    assert_equal(Tactics::LOSS, Tactics.new(0b1111_1011_1111_1111).play)
    assert_equal(Tactics::LOSS, Tactics.new(0b1111_1101_1111_1111).play)
    assert_equal(Tactics::LOSS, Tactics.new(0b1111_1110_1111_1111).play)
    assert_equal(Tactics::LOSS, Tactics.new(0b1111_1111_0111_1111).play)
    assert_equal(Tactics::LOSS, Tactics.new(0b1111_1111_1011_1111).play)
    assert_equal(Tactics::LOSS, Tactics.new(0b1111_1111_1101_1111).play)
    assert_equal(Tactics::LOSS, Tactics.new(0b1111_1111_1110_1111).play)
    assert_equal(Tactics::LOSS, Tactics.new(0b1111_1111_1111_0111).play)
    assert_equal(Tactics::LOSS, Tactics.new(0b1111_1111_1111_1011).play)
    assert_equal(Tactics::LOSS, Tactics.new(0b1111_1111_1111_1101).play)
    assert_equal(Tactics::LOSS, Tactics.new(0b1111_1111_1111_1110).play)

    # 2 squares in a row wins (because you can reduce to one square)
    assert_equal(Tactics::WIN, Tactics.new(0b0011_1111_1111_1111).play)
    assert_equal(Tactics::WIN, Tactics.new(0b1001_1111_1111_1111).play)
    assert_equal(Tactics::WIN, Tactics.new(0b1100_1111_1111_1111).play)
```

```
assert_equal(Tactics::WIN, Tactics.new(0b1111_0011_1111_1111).play)
assert_equal(Tactics::WIN, Tactics.new(0b1111_1001_1111_1111).play)
assert_equal(Tactics::WIN, Tactics.new(0b1111_1100_1111_1111).play)

assert_equal(Tactics::WIN, Tactics.new(0b1111_1111_0011_1111).play)
assert_equal(Tactics::WIN, Tactics.new(0b1111_1111_1001_1111).play)
assert_equal(Tactics::WIN, Tactics.new(0b1111_1111_1100_1111).play)

assert_equal(Tactics::WIN, Tactics.new(0b1111_1111_1111_0011).play)
assert_equal(Tactics::WIN, Tactics.new(0b1111_1111_1111_1001).play)
assert_equal(Tactics::WIN, Tactics.new(0b1111_1111_1111_1100).play)

assert_equal(Tactics::WIN, Tactics.new(0b0111_0111_1111_1111).play)
assert_equal(Tactics::WIN, Tactics.new(0b1111_0111_0111_1111).play)
assert_equal(Tactics::WIN, Tactics.new(0b1111_1111_0111_0111).play)

assert_equal(Tactics::WIN, Tactics.new(0b1011_1011_1111_1111).play)
assert_equal(Tactics::WIN, Tactics.new(0b1111_1011_1011_1111).play)
assert_equal(Tactics::WIN, Tactics.new(0b1111_1111_1011_1011).play)

assert_equal(Tactics::WIN, Tactics.new(0b1101_1101_1111_1111).play)
assert_equal(Tactics::WIN, Tactics.new(0b1111_1101_1101_1111).play)
assert_equal(Tactics::WIN, Tactics.new(0b1111_1111_1101_1101).play)

assert_equal(Tactics::WIN, Tactics.new(0b1110_1110_1111_1111).play)
assert_equal(Tactics::WIN, Tactics.new(0b1111_1110_1110_1111).play)
assert_equal(Tactics::WIN, Tactics.new(0b1111_1111_1110_1110).play)

# 3 squares in a row wins (because you can reduce to one square)

assert_equal(Tactics::WIN, Tactics.new(0b0001_1111_1111_1111).play)
assert_equal(Tactics::WIN, Tactics.new(0b1000_1111_1111_1111).play)

assert_equal(Tactics::WIN, Tactics.new(0b1111_0001_1111_1111).play)
assert_equal(Tactics::WIN, Tactics.new(0b1111_1000_1111_1111).play)

assert_equal(Tactics::WIN, Tactics.new(0b1111_1111_0001_1111).play)
assert_equal(Tactics::WIN, Tactics.new(0b1111_1111_1000_1111).play)

assert_equal(Tactics::WIN, Tactics.new(0b1111_1111_1111_0001).play)
assert_equal(Tactics::WIN, Tactics.new(0b1111_1111_1111_1000).play)


assert_equal(Tactics::WIN, Tactics.new(0b0111_0111_0111_1111).play)
assert_equal(Tactics::WIN, Tactics.new(0b1111_0111_0111_0111).play)

assert_equal(Tactics::WIN, Tactics.new(0b1011_1011_1011_1111).play)
assert_equal(Tactics::WIN, Tactics.new(0b1111_1011_1011_1011).play)


assert_equal(Tactics::WIN, Tactics.new(0b1101_1101_1101_1111).play)
```

```
assert_equal(Tactics::WIN, Tactics.new(0b1111_1101_1101_1101).play)

assert_equal(Tactics::WIN, Tactics.new(0b1110_1110_1110_1111).play)
assert_equal(Tactics::WIN, Tactics.new(0b1111_1110_1110_1110).play)

# 4 squares in a row wins (because you can reduce to one square)

assert_equal(Tactics::WIN, Tactics.new(0b0000_1111_1111_1111).play)
assert_equal(Tactics::WIN, Tactics.new(0b1111_0000_1111_1111).play)
assert_equal(Tactics::WIN, Tactics.new(0b1111_1111_0000_1111).play)
assert_equal(Tactics::WIN, Tactics.new(0b1111_1111_1111_0000).play)

assert_equal(Tactics::WIN, Tactics.new(0b0111_0111_0111_0111).play)
assert_equal(Tactics::WIN, Tactics.new(0b1011_1011_1011_1011).play)
assert_equal(Tactics::WIN, Tactics.new(0b1101_1101_1101_1101).play)
assert_equal(Tactics::WIN, Tactics.new(0b1110_1110_1110_1110).play)

# 2x2 square loses (because your opponent can always reduce it to one
# square immediately after your move)
assert_equal(Tactics::LOSS, Tactics.new(0b0011_0011_1111_1111).play)
assert_equal(Tactics::LOSS, Tactics.new(0b1111_0011_0011_1111).play)
assert_equal(Tactics::LOSS, Tactics.new(0b1111_1111_0011_0011).play)

assert_equal(Tactics::LOSS, Tactics.new(0b1001_1001_1111_1111).play)
assert_equal(Tactics::LOSS, Tactics.new(0b1111_1001_1001_1111).play)
assert_equal(Tactics::LOSS, Tactics.new(0b1111_1111_1001_1001).play)

assert_equal(Tactics::LOSS, Tactics.new(0b1100_1100_1111_1111).play)
assert_equal(Tactics::LOSS, Tactics.new(0b1111_1100_1100_1111).play)
assert_equal(Tactics::LOSS, Tactics.new(0b1111_1111_1100_1100).play)

# 2x3 (or 3x2) rectangle wins (because you can reduce it to a 2x2)
assert_equal(Tactics::WIN, Tactics.new(0b0011_0011_0011_1111).play)
assert_equal(Tactics::WIN, Tactics.new(0b1001_1001_1001_1111).play)

assert_equal(Tactics::WIN, Tactics.new(0b1100_1100_1100_1111).play)
assert_equal(Tactics::WIN, Tactics.new(0b1111_0011_0011_0011).play)

assert_equal(Tactics::WIN, Tactics.new(0b1111_1001_1001_1001).play)
assert_equal(Tactics::WIN, Tactics.new(0b1111_1100_1100_1100).play)

assert_equal(Tactics::WIN, Tactics.new(0b0001_0001_1111_1111).play)
assert_equal(Tactics::WIN, Tactics.new(0b1000_1000_1111_1111).play)

assert_equal(Tactics::WIN, Tactics.new(0b1111_0001_0001_1111).play)
assert_equal(Tactics::WIN, Tactics.new(0b1111_1000_1000_1111).play)

assert_equal(Tactics::WIN, Tactics.new(0b1111_1111_0001_0001).play)
assert_equal(Tactics::WIN, Tactics.new(0b1111_1111_1000_1000).play)

# Now we'll play from an empty board. The purpose of this assertion
```

```
    # is just to verify that we get the same answer that we get when
    # the engine is started from scratch. In this case, we have done all the
    # preceding plays-the results of which are stored in the engine.
    assert_equal(Tactics::LOSS, Tactics.new(0b0000_0000_0000_0000).play)

    # Also check that it works the same with the defaulted empty board.
    assert_equal(Tactics::LOSS, Tactics.new.play)

    # Continue with a few random assertions. No attempt to be exhaustive
    # this time. This is deliberately located below the full play, above,
    # to see that intermediate board positions that have been stored
    # are accurate. Of course, this doesn't test very many of them.

    # A 2x2 L shape. Trivially reducible to 1 square.
    assert_equal(Tactics::WIN, Tactics.new(0b0011_0111_1111_1111).play)
    assert_equal(Tactics::WIN, Tactics.new(0b1111_1011_1001_1111).play)

    # A 2x3 L shape. Trivially reducible to 1 square.
    assert_equal(Tactics::WIN, Tactics.new(0b0011_0111_0111_1111).play)
    assert_equal(Tactics::WIN, Tactics.new(0b1111_1011_1000_1111).play)

    # A 2x4 L shape. Trivially reducible to 1 square.
    assert_equal(Tactics::WIN, Tactics.new(0b0011_0111_0111_0111).play)
    assert_equal(Tactics::WIN, Tactics.new(0b1111_0111_0000_1111).play)

    # A 3x4 L shape. Reducible to two lengths of two.
    assert_equal(Tactics::WIN, Tactics.new(0b0001_0111_0111_0111).play)
    assert_equal(Tactics::WIN, Tactics.new(0b0000_0111_0111_1111).play)

    # A checkerboard. Wins as long as the number of open squares is even.
    assert_equal(Tactics::WIN, Tactics.new(0b0101_1010_0101_1010).play)
    assert_equal(Tactics::WIN, Tactics.new(0b1010_0101_1010_0101).play)
  end
end
```

That's a flawless combination of code and comment logic, if you ask me. With these tests, Bob is verifying everything he can prove by hand. If his engine agrees in all of these cases, it will be hard to question its judgment.

Additional Exercises

1. Write some code to validate the perfect-play strategy at the beginning of this discussion. (Hint: Bob already did most of the work for you.)

2. Write some code to prove that a 4×2 board yields the same results as a 4×4 board. (Hint: Again, you can solve this by taking another page out of Bob's book.)

Cryptograms

Odds are that if you tried a brute-force approach, you didn't get very far. Quiz creator Glenn P. Parker explains why that is:

> Solving a cryptogram by brute force is prohibitively expensive. The maximum number of possible solutions is 26!, or roughly 4×10^{26}, so the first challenge is to pare down the search to something manageable.

The size of the search space makes this problem quite challenging. Glenn's own solution has trouble with some inputs. Glenn didn't wait on it to finish crypto3.txt, for example, because it may take days to solve that one. However, the code is still useful, and I want to take a closer look at it.

Using Word Signatures

First, let's take a look at Glenn's explanation of how the code works:

> My solution begins with the insight that any word, either a regular dictionary word or a cryptographic token, can be viewed as a pattern of repeated and nonrepeated characters. For example, banana has the pattern [1 2 3 2 3 2], where the first letter is used exactly once, the second letter is used three times, and the third letter is used twice. These patterns group all known words into families. The word banana belongs to the same family as the word rococo.

> All words in a dictionary can be grouped into families according to their patterns, and each cryptographic token has its own pattern that corresponds (with any luck) to one of the families from the dictionary. If a token has no matching family, then it cannot be solved with the given dictionary, so we won't worry about that case too much.

Let's dive right in and look at Glenn's dictionary code:

`code/cryptograms/crypto.rb`

```ruby
STDOUT.sync = true

# A utility class to read files containing words one-per-line
class WordReader
  include Enumerable
  def initialize(filename)
    @filename = filename
  end
  def each
    File.open(@filename) do |file|
      file.each do |word|
        word.chomp!
        next if word.length == 0
        yield word
      end
    end
  end
end


# A copy of the dictionary, with words grouped by "signature".
# A signature simplifies a word to its repeating letter patterns.
# The signature for "cat" is 1.2.3 because each successive letter
# in cat is unique.  The signature for "banana" is 1.2.3.2.3.2,
# where letter 2, "a", is repeated three times and letter 3, "n"
# is repeated twice.
class Dictionary
  def initialize(filename)
    @all = {}
    @sigs = {}

    WordReader.new(filename).each { |word|
      word.downcase!
      word.gsub!(/[^a-z]/, '')
      next if word.empty?
      @all[word] = true
      sig = signature(word)
      @sigs[sig] ||= []
      @sigs[sig].push(word)
    }
    self.freeze
  end

  def lookup(word)
    @all[word]
  end

  def candidates(cipher)
    @sigs[signature(cipher)]
  end
```

```
  private

  def signature(word)
    seen = {}
    u = 0
    sig = []
    word.each_byte do |b|
      if not seen[b]
        u += 1
        seen[b] = u
      end
      sig.push(seen[b])
    end
    sig.join('.')
  end
end
```

As the comment says, WordReader is a helper class that allows you to iterate over a word file without worrying about annoyances like calling chomp() for every line. The main work method here is each(), which will provide callers with one word from the file at a time. WordReader includes Enumerable to gain access to all the other standard iterators. The file name must be set with object construction.

The word file is wrapped in a Dictionary object. As Glenn explained, it maps words based on their signature(). If you glance down at that method, you will see that it performs the conversion Glenn described.

The initialize() method puts this converter and WordReader to use by transferring the word file into its own internal representation. Words are stored both normally in @all and by signature family in @sigs.

The final two methods allow user code to query the Dictionary. lookup() tells you whether a word is in the Dictionary, and, candidates(), returns an array containing the family of words matching the signature of the provided word.

Building the Map

Let's go back to Glenn for an explanation of the rest of his algorithm:

> We start by assuming that one of the cryptographic tokens corresponds to one of the words in its family. This pairing produces a partial map of input to output characters. So, if we examine the token, xyzyzy, we might assume that it is really the word banana. The partial map that results is x->b y->a z->n, or the following:

```
abcdefghijklmnopqrstuvwxyz
.....................ban
```

Note that this mapping will affect all other cryptographic tokens that share the letters x, y, and z. In fact, it may even solve some of them completely (as zyx becomes nab, for example). Or, the map may convert another token into a word that is not in the dictionary, so zyxxyz becomes nabban, which is not in my dictionary. This is a useful trick that will reduce the size of the search.

Next we assume that another token can be mapped into a dictionary word from its family, which produces another partial map that must be combined with the first map. This combination can fail in two ways. First, the new map may have a previously mapped input letter going to a different output letter, so if we mapped uvwxyz to monkey, the result would be a map where x mapped to both b and k. Second, the new map may have a previously unused input letter going to an output letter that was already used, so if we mapped abcdef to monkey, the result would map both c and z to n. Failed mappings also serve to reduce the size of the search.

For my solution, I used a depth-first search, working through the tokens and trying every word in its family. The tokens are ordered according to increasing family size, so the tokens with the fewest possible solutions are examined first. At each level of the recursion, all the words for a token are applied in sequence to the current map. If the resulting map is valid, I recurse, and the new map is applied to the remaining unsolved tokens to see whether they are already solved or unsolvable. Solved tokens are ignored for the rest of this branch of the search, and unsolvable tokens are shelved. Then I start working on the next token with the new map.

The recursion terminates when a complete map is found, the number of shelved (unsolvable) tokens exceeds a limit, or every family word has been used for the last token.

We are interested in maps that do not yield dictionary words for every token. This is because cryptograms often contain nondictionary words, so we may be satisfied by a partial solution even when a full solution is impossible. Finding partial solutions is more expensive than finding only full solutions, since the search space can be significantly larger. Aside from the trick of shelving unsolvable words, partial solutions require us to selectively ignore tokens that may be "spoiling" the search even though they produce valid maps. My solution does not fully implement this.

There's plenty of code to go along with the explanation, but we will work through it a piece at a time. Here's the map class that manages the translation from puzzle (or cipher text) to answer (or plain text):

```code/cryptograms/crypto.rb```

```ruby
# CMap maintains the mapping from cipher text to plain text and
# some state related to the solution.  @map is the actual mapping.
# @solved is just a string with all the solved words.  @shelved
# is an array of cipher text words that cannot be solved because
# the current mapping resolves all their letters and the result
# is not found in the dictionary.
class CMap
  attr_reader :map, :solved, :shelved

  def initialize(arg = nil, newmap = nil, dword = nil)
    case
    when arg.kind_of?(String)
      @map = arg.dup
    when arg.kind_of?(CMap)
      @map = newmap || arg.map.dup
      @solved = arg.solved.dup
      @shelved = arg.shelved.dup
      append_solved(dword) if dword
    else
      @map = '.' * 26
      @solved = ''
      @shelved = []
    end
  end

  def dup
    CMap.new(self)
  end

  # Attempt to update the map to include all letter combinations
  # needed to map cword into dword.  Return nil if a conflict is found.
  def learn(cword, dword)
    newmap = @map.dup
    (0...cword.length).each do |i|
      c = cword[i] - ?a
      p = newmap[c]
      # check for correct mapping
      next if p == dword[i]
      # check for incorrect mapping
      return nil if (p != ?.) || newmap.include?(dword[i])
      # create new mapping
      newmap[c] = dword[i]
    end
    CMap.new(self, newmap, dword)
  end

  def append_solved(dword)
    @solved += ' ' unless @solved.empty?
    @solved += dword
  end
```
```

```
    def shelve(cword)
      @shelved << cword
    end

    def convert(cword)
      pattern = ''
      cword.each_byte do |c|
        pattern << @map[c - ?a]
      end
      pattern
    end
end
```

The comments are strong here and should give you a great idea of what is going on in initialize() and learn(), the two tricky methods. The standard initialize() is really three constructors in one. It can be passed a String mapping, a CMap object (copy constructor used by dup()), or nothing at all. Each branch of the **case** handles one of those conditions by setting instance variables as described in the comment.

The other method doing heavy work is learn(). Given a cipher word and a dictionary word, it updates a copy of its current mapping, character by character. The process is aborted (and **nil** returned) if the method finds that a provided character has already been mapped. Otherwise, learn returns the newly constructed CMap object.

The methods append_solved() and shelve() both add words to the indicated listing. Finally, convert() uses the mapping to convert a provided cipher word. The return value will have known letters switched and contain . characters as placeholders for unknown letters.

Assembling a Solution

The next class wraps those tools up into a solution:

`code/cryptograms/crypto.rb`
```
class Cryptogram
  def initialize(filename, dict)
    @dict = dict
    @words = WordReader.new(filename).to_a
    # clist is the input cipher with no duplicated words
    # and no unrecognized input characters
    @clist = []
    @words.each do |word|
      word.downcase!
      word.gsub!(/[^a-z]/, '')
      next if word.empty? || @clist.include?(word)
      @clist.push(word)
    end
```

```
        # Sort by increasing size of candidate list
        @clist = @clist.sort_by {|w| @dict.candidates(w).length}
    end
end
```

The constructor is mainly responsible for reading Cryptogram. It uses WordReader(), adding each normalized word to an internal cipher list.

`code/cryptograms/crypto.rb`
```ruby
class Cryptogram
  def solve(max_unsolved = 0, stop_on_first = true)
    @max_unsolved = max_unsolved
    @stop_on_first = stop_on_first
    @checks = 0
    @solutions = {}
    @partials = {}
    solve_p(@clist, CMap.new, 0)
  end

  def solve_p(list, cmap, depth)
    # Simplify list if possible
    list = prescreen(list, cmap)
    return if check_solution(list, cmap)
    solve_r(list, cmap, depth)
    return if done?
  end#solve_p

  def solve_r(start_list, start_cmap, depth)
    for i in (0...start_list.length)
      # Pull a cword out of start_list
      list = start_list.dup
      cword = list.delete_at(i)

      pattern = start_cmap.convert(cword)
      search(cword, pattern) do |dword|
        # Try to make a new cmap by learning dword for cword
        next unless cmap = start_cmap.learn(cword, dword)
        # Recurse on remaining words
        solve_p(list, cmap, depth + 1)
        return if done?
      end#search
    end#for
  end#solve_r

  def done?
    @stop_on_first && @solutions.length > 0
  end
```

```
# Return the subset of cwords in list that are not fully solved by cmap.
# Update cmap with learned and shelved words.
def prescreen(list, cmap)
  start_list = []
  list.each do |cword|
    pattern = cmap.convert(cword)
    if pattern.include?(?.)
      # cword was not fully resolved.
      start_list << cword
    elsif @dict.lookup(pattern)
      # cword was resolved and is a known word.
      cmap.learn(cword, pattern)
    else
      # cword cannot be solved.
      cmap.shelve(cword)
    end
  end
  start_list
end
end
```

The methods solve(), solve_p(), and solve_r() are three pieces of one process. The interface is solve(), and it sets up a handful of instance variables to track its work on the solution. A handoff is then made to solve_p(), which makes a prescreening attempt to simplify the list. When the list is ready, the work is again passed to solve_r(). That method iterates over the unknown words, trying to find matches for them and updating the map based on those matches. At each step, it passes the remaining list back to solve_p() (indirect recursion). This process repeats until either method detects an end condition.

The done?() method is the check used to stop processing by solve_p() and solve_r(). It just verifies that a solution has been found and we don't want to continue looking for more.

Indirectly, solve_p() uses prescreen() to trim the list. The method just walks the word list using the current map to convert the words. Words are fed to the map to learn if they are in the dictionary, kept in the working list whether they're partially solved, and shelved if they cannot be solved with this dictionary.

code/cryptograms/crypto.rb
```
class Cryptogram
  # Generate dictionary words matching the pattern
  def search(cword, pattern)
    # the pattern will normally have at least one unknown character
    if pattern.include? ?.
      re = Regexp.new("^#{pattern}$")
```

```
        @dict.candidates(cword).each do |dword|
          yield dword if re =~ dword
        end
      # otherwise, just check that the pattern is actually a known word.
      elsif @dict.lookup(pattern)
        yield pattern
      end
    end
  end
end
```

The search() method is used in solve_r() to iterate over a dictionary family by pattern. You give search() a cipher word and a pattern from the current map, and it will **yield** to the provided block all candidate words for the cipher word matching the pattern. This is why patterns use dots for unknown letters; it's a direct Regexp translation.

`code/cryptograms/crypto.rb`
```ruby
class Cryptogram
  def check_solution(list, cmap)
    @checks += 1
    unsolved = list.length + cmap.shelved.length

    # Did we get lucky?
    if unsolved == 0
      if not @solutions.has_key?(cmap.map)
        @solutions[cmap.map] = true
        if not @stop_on_first
          puts "\nfound complete solution \##{@solutions.length}"
          puts "performed #{@checks} checks"
          show_cmap(cmap)
        end
      end
      return true
    end

    # Give up if too many words cannot be solved
    return true if cmap.shelved.length > @max_unsolved

    # Check for satisfactory partial solution
    if unsolved <= @max_unsolved
      if not @partials.has_key?(cmap.map)
        @partials[cmap.map] = true
        puts "\nfound partial \##{@partials.length} with #{unsolved} unsolved"
        puts "performed #{@checks} checks"
        puts Time.now
        show_cmap(cmap)
      end
    end
    return false
  end
end
```

The last real work method is check_solution(). It examines the current word list and map to see whether a solution has been found. That can be true if all words have been completed, there are too many unknowns and we are forced to give up, or we're in an acceptable range of unknown (or partially solved) words. The method returns a **true** or **false** answer.

`code/cryptograms/crypto.rb`

```ruby
class Cryptogram
  def show
    puts "Performed #{@checks} checks"
    puts "Found #{@solutions.length} solutions"
    @solutions.each_key { |sol| show_cmap(CMap.new(sol)) }
    puts
    puts "Found #{@partials.length} partial solutions"
    @partials.each_key  { |sol| show_cmap(CMap.new(sol)) }
  end

  def show_cmap(cmap)
    puts(('a'..'z').to_a.join(''))
    puts cmap.map
    puts
    @words.each do |word|
      pattern = cmap.convert(word)
      printf "%-20s %s %-20s\n", word,
             (@dict.lookup(pattern) ? ' ' : '*'), pattern
    end
    puts '-' * 42
  end
end
```

The last two methods, show() and show_cmap(), are just utility methods for printing a result set to the terminal.

Finally, here's the last little piece of code that starts the process:

`code/cryptograms/crypto.rb`

```ruby
DICTFILE = ARGV[0]
PARTIAL = ARGV[1].to_i

puts "Reading dictionary #{DICTFILE}"
dict = Dictionary.new(DICTFILE)

ARGV[2..-1].each do |filename|
  puts "Solving cryptogram #{filename} allowing #{PARTIAL} unknowns", Time.now
  cryp = Cryptogram.new(filename, dict)
  cryp.solve PARTIAL
  puts "Cryptogram solution", Time.now
  cryp.show
end
```

This chunk of code is really just processing command-line arguments. The dictionary file is read along with the number of allowed partials (words not in the dictionary). The rest of the arguments are filtered through the Cryptogram class, and the results are shown to the user.

A Look at Limitations

This solution has a few problems. If you play around with the code, you'll notice that speed is one of them. There's a lot of data to churn through, and although the script displays some results quickly, it can take it some time to present a final answer. Luckily, the early work is usually close enough that the user can easily fill in the blanks.

The other problem I'll leave to Glenn to explain:

> *The weakness in my approach is that tokens are always added to the solution using a single, predefined order. But the tokens that are mixed in first can have an overwhelming influence on the final maps that result. In the worst case, the first token to be mapped can make it impossible to add any other tokens to the map.*
>
> *The only solution I know is to add another wrapper around the entire search process that mutates the order of the token mixing.*

Additional Exercises

1. Implement the wrapper to fix the order problem Glenn describes.

2. Enhance your own code, or Glenn's code, with a vowel check during mapping. Assume that all words contain at least one *a, e, i, o, u,* or *y.*

3. Solve a cryptogram without the help of a computer. You can find a nice collection by difficulty online at http://www.oneacross.com/cryptograms/.

Appendix A

Resources

A.1 Bibliography

[Ste00]   Neal Stephenson. *Cryptonomicon*. Perennial, 2000.

[Tzu05]   Sun Tzu. *The Art of War, Special Edition*. El Paso Norte Press, 2005.

Index

D

Facets of Ruby Series

Now that you're a Ruby programmer, you'll want the definitive book on the Ruby language. Learn how to use Ruby to write exciting new applications. And if you're thinking of using Ruby to create Web applications, you really need to look at Ruby on Rails.

Programming Ruby (The PickAxe)

• The definitive guide for Ruby programmers. • Up-to-date and expanded for Ruby version 1.8. • Complete documentation of all the built-in classes, modules, and methods. • Complete descriptions of all ninety-eight standard libraries. • 200+ pages of new content in this edition. • Learn more about Ruby's web tools, unit testing, and programming philosophy.

Programming Ruby: **The Pragmatic Programmer's Guide, 2nd Edition**
Dave Thomas with Chad Fowler and Andy Hunt
(864 pages) ISBN: 0-9745140-5-5. $44.95

Agile Web Development with Rails

• The definitive guide for Rails developers. • Tutorial introduction, and in-depth reference. • All the scoop on ActiveRecord, ActionPack, and ActionView. • Special *David Says...* content by the inventor of Rails. • Chapters on testing, web services, Ajax, security, e-mail, deployment, and more.

Agile Web Development with Rails
Dave Thomas and David Heinemeier Hansson, with Leon Breedt, Mike Clark, Thomas Fuchs, and Andreas Schwarz
(560 pages) ISBN: 0-9745140-0-X. $34.95

The Pragmatic Bookshelf

The Pragmatic Bookshelf features books written by developers for developers. The titles continue the well-known Pragmatic Programmer style, and continue to garner awards and rave reviews. As development gets more and more difficult, the Pragmatic Programmers will be there with more titles and products to help programmers stay on top of their game.

Visit Us Online

Best of Ruby Quiz
pragmaticprogrammer.com/titles/fr_quiz
Source code from this book, errata, and other resources. Come give us feedback, too!

Register for Updates
pragmaticprogrammer.com/updates
Be notified when updates and new books become available.

Join the Community
pragmaticprogrammer.com/community
Read our weblogs, join our online discussions, participate in our mailing list, interact with our wiki, and benefit from the experience of other Pragmatic Programmers.

New and Noteworthy
pragmaticprogrammer.com/news
Check out the latest pragmatic developments in the news.

Save on the PDF and other Ruby Books

Save more than 60% on the PDF version of this book. Owning the paper version of this book entitles you to purchase the PDF version for only $5.00 (regularly $13.00). That's a saving of more than 60%. The PDF is great for carrying around on your laptop. It's hyperlinked, has color, and is fully searchable. Buy it now at pragmaticprogrammer.com/coupon

Contact Us

Phone Orders:	1-800-699-PROG (+1 919 847 3884)
Online Orders:	www.pragmaticprogrammer.com/catalog
Customer Service:	orders@pragmaticprogrammer.com
Non-English Versions:	translations@pragmaticprogrammer.com
Pragmatic Teaching:	academic@pragmaticprogrammer.com
Author Proposals:	proposals@pragmaticprogrammer.com